REBEL ASSAULT™

THE OFFICIAL INSIDER'S GUIDE

Other Prima Game Books Available Now!

X-Wing: The Official Strategy Guide
The Official Lucasfilm Games Air Combat Strategies Book
Wing Commander I and II: The Ultimate Strategy Guide
Master of Orion: The Official Strategy Guide
Outpost: The Official Strategy Guide
JetFighter II: The Official Strategy Guide
Chuck Yeager's Air Combat Handbook
Dynamix Great War Planes: The Ultimate Strategy Guide
F-15 Strike Eagle III: The Official Strategy Guide (with disk)
Microsoft Flight Simulator: The Official Strategy Guide
Strike Commander: The Official Strategy Guide and Flight School
Falcon 3: The Official Combat Strategy Book, revised ed.
Aces Over Europe: The Official Strategy Guide
Stunt Island: The Official Strategy Guide
The 7th Guest: The Official Strategy Guide
Myst: The Official Strategy Guide
Return to Zork Adventurer's Guide
CD-ROM Games Secrets, Volume 1

How to Order:

Individual orders and quantity discounts are available from the publisher, Prima Publishing, P.O. Box 1260BK, Rocklin, CA 95677; phone: 916-632-4400. On your letterhead include information concerning the intended use of the books and the number of books you wish to purchase. Turn to the back of this book for more information.

REBEL
ASSAULT™
THE OFFICIAL INSIDER'S GUIDE

Joe Hutsko

Prima Publishing
P.O. Box 1260BK
Rocklin, CA 95677

Secrets of the Games is an imprint of Prima Publishing, Rocklin, California 95677.

Publisher, Entertainment Division: Roger Stewart
Managing Editor: Paula Munier Lee
Project Editor: Dan J. Foster
Book Design and Production: Danielle Foster, Scribe Tribe
Cover Production Coordinator: Anne Flemke
Photography: Mary Merrick and Lucasfilm Ltd. All rights reserved.
Cover Design Adaptation: The Dunlavey Studio

ISBN: 1-55958-789-X
Library of Congress Catalog Card Number: 94-66678
Printed in the United States of America
94 95 96 97 CWO 10 9 8 7 6 5 4 3 2 1

For
Michael J. Hartman

Contents

Part III   The Crunch   51

Acknowledgments

LIKE REBEL ASSAULT ITSELF, creating this book required the effort of more than just the person whose name appears on the cover.

At the top of the list, thanks to Roger Stewart of Prima Publishing for taking me under his publishing wing, and to Matt Wagner, my *primo* agent at Waterside Productions, who put Roger and me in touch in the first place. Thanks also to Prima's Diane Pasquetti and to Waterside's Bill Gladstone, Carol Underwood, and Lavander Ginsberg, each for their ceaseless professionalism, support, and, above all else, courtesy. Thanks also to Danielle Foster, who designed and produced this book.

More Prima kudos go to my editor, Dan Foster, who presented a cool head and a warm welcome throughout the project, and to Neweleen Trebnik, a production sovereign every publisher should be so lucky to have. Thanks also to Michael Van Mantgem, copywriter by day, novelist by night.

At LucasArts, thanks to everyone I interviewed for this book, especially Vince Lee and Ron Lussier, and to those who, while they may not have gone on record between these covers, were equally helpful in getting this thing done—especially Camela Boswell and Judy Allen, who ushered photographer Mary Merrick and me through several whirlwind point-and-shoot sessions. Extra thanks to Mary Bihr, who acted as my friendly, one-stop LucasArts contact from start to finish, and to Amanda Haverlock, for putting through with good humor and grace my constant calls to the company.

At Lucasfilm Ltd., special thanks to Lucy Autrey Wilson, who gave this book the go-ahead in the first place, and to Sue Rostoni, who led me to the company's extensive photo archive, from which I selected the storyboards, sketches, and various other *Star Wars* artworks that so boldly adorn these pages.

On the hardware side of things, Devorah Symansky and Megan Manning of Copithorne & Bellows and Lucy Honig and Mattie Kirby of Hewlett-Packard kindly loaned me an HP OmniBook 425 subnotebook computer, which made my back-and-forth bus rides between San Francisco and San Rafael all the more productive; and Michael Velasco at Golin–Harris and Jan Rasmussen at NEC loaned me a super-speedy NEC MultiSpin 3Xp CD-ROM. Thanks, folks.

Mary Merrick, who captured the Rebel Assault cast of characters so distinctly, is a close friend and a joy to work with. Her sharp and sometimes twisted sense of humor more than once shed a humorous light on this whole making-of-the-making-of project, and for that I am very grateful. ("There ought to be a law!")

Thanks to Rich Mason, whose *Starfighter Command*, a Windows-based, electronic magazine published quarterly in CompuServe's Flight Sim Forum, offered deep insight into the mind of a dedicated *Star Wars* junky and his take on Rebel Assault.

Last, though far from least, special thanks to my family and friends, who are the best a guy could ask for. One friend in particular, who put up with what I suppose you'd call the fleeting manic-depressive moods a writer swings between when he's doing his thing, was especially supportive—*mi mejor amigo*, Drew.

Introduction

HAVE YOU EVER WONDERED HOW A MULTIMEDIA GAME IS CREATED? You're about to find out. And this is not about just any multimedia game, but the best-selling CD-ROM game ever—Rebel Assault, by LucasArts Entertainment Company. Started over a decade ago by writer/director/ producer George Lucas, LucasArts has both feet firmly planted in that actualized place referred to as "Digital Hollywood"—where dynamic digital technologies merge with the cinematic storytelling of Hollywood to create a whole new genre of entertainment.

Modeled after the "making of" type of movie book, this book shows you what takes place on the other side of the screen, behind the scenes. From start-up to stores' shelves, it's all here—the complete inside story of how a group of bright and talented people produced the first CD-ROM game based in the *Star Wars* universe.

You will see, in detailed illustrations and photographs, and hear, in the Rebel Assault team's own words, precisely how this ground-breaking title was born. From the whiz-kid programmers to the stylish 3-D artist/ animators; from the scrupulous, untiring playtesters to those unsung he-roes on the other end of the phone line, the Product Support folks, this high-tech cast of characters weaves each piece of the Rebel Assault puzzle into a compelling and sometimes dramatic story.

How you approach this book is up to you. Like a general nonfiction title, this text is meant to be read for pleasure. Like a picture book, its many photos and illustrations are meant to be examined and enjoyed. Hopefully, your excursion between these covers will be an entertaining and educational one.

For you dedicated *Star Wars* fans, you'll be pleased to see more than forty pieces of art taken directly from the Lucasfilm *Star Wars* film archives. The Rebel Assault team had its share of *Star Wars* aficionados who studied these very same artworks and then brought them to spinning life in the CD-ROM to which this book is dedicated.

Have I forgotten anyone?... Oh, yes—you may have picked up this book for its dazzling 16-page color section. Indeed, it's hard not to notice that first. This special color section not only follows the Rebel Assault story-line chapter by chapter, but it is also filled with secret Rebel Assault player cheat codes and strategy tips that will help you beat the Evil Empire at its own sly tricks.

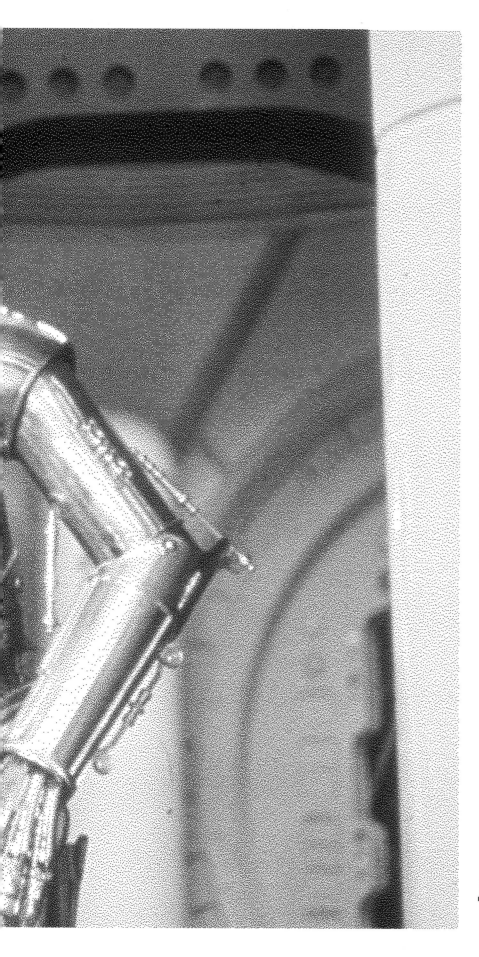

ONE

A (Not So) Long
Time Ago…

...TWO AND A HALF YEARS AGO, TO BE EXACT, Vince Lee, a 24-year-old programmer, attended the Winter Consumer Electronics Show (CES) in Chicago with several of his LucasArts associates.

What they saw at that show—the development of the electronic entertainment industry and its associated technologies and the inventive and compelling game titles that were being released—encouraged LucasArts executives to pursue a notion they had been tossing around for some time—the creation of a 3-D CD-ROM game based on the *Star Wars* world.

Vince Lee: Boy Wonder

But which of their employees, the executives wondered, could undertake the research and development of such a dynamic and ambitious title? Enter Vince Lee.

"I considered myself pretty green," says Vince, who, a year before that Winter '92 CES, had come to LucasArts straight from the University of California at Berkeley, where he had earned his Master's degree in Robotics. "I'd done some programming in my spare time, and I'd played games, but not LucasArts's in particular. One day I met a LucasArts

Vince Lee, Rebel Assault's designer, programmer, and project leader.

The main lobby at LucasArts's San Rafael, California, headquarters.

producer at a User's Group meeting who suggested I call him when I graduated. So I did." Invited to LucasArts's San Rafael, California, offices for an interview, Vince says he was so impressed by the creative, laid-back atmosphere that he had no trouble turning down Exxon and IBM, both of which had offered him jobs in mechanical engineering, in favor of a programming job with the interactive game company.

Working as a programmer, Vince spent most of his time creating various art and animation tools that LucasArts game designers used to convert several of the company's popular PC-based graphic adventure games into Amiga versions. He was working on the Amiga version of Indiana Jones and the Fate of Atlantis when the general manager of LucasArts suggested him as the programmer for the proposed 3-D CD-ROM *Star Wars* project. Although the company had recently entered the CD-ROM realm with its talkie graphic adventures (CD-ROM versions of existing, floppy-based titles whose characters spoke their dialog in recorded human voices that players would hear rather than read as on-screen text), Vince's project, as it was to become known, marked the company's first-ever foray into the creation of a title exclusively for CD-ROM.

The company knew it wanted to base its first CD-ROM-exclusive game on *Star Wars* six months before the Rebel Assault project took off.

Rebel Risks

Jack Sorensen, Director of Business Operations, says that the decision to use the *Star Wars* property was made six months before Vince was called in. "The design went through four or five configurations," like a Hollywood film script. "The technology was so new," he says, that it meant facing questions such as "What kinds of games work on what platforms? Could it be ported to other platforms? At the time, platforms like Sega CD didn't have development systems yet." In part, these questions were what prompted LucasArts management to consider Vince in the first place. "We needed someone who had a good gaming sense. There was going to be a lot of development and a lot of designing during development, so using someone who was actually doing the technology was the only way this thing was going to get some direction." Otherwise, they feared, the team would have to keep redesigning the game as they learned more about the technology.

At first, Vince says, the idea was vague. "They said, 'make it a *Star Wars*-based game, but have it more land-based, with some flying over terrain, as opposed to all space,' which is what X-Wing was at the time."

With that open-ended mandate, Vince set about defining the scope of the project. "I was thinking: What's the advantage of CD-ROM? We wanted to do a game that would be the type of game you could only do with CD-ROM." Vince says that the space a CD-ROM provides (about 600MB, the equivalent of about 425 floppy disks) was a big factor, because it would enable him to incorporate lots of non-repetitive imagery.

All of that space loaded with lots of lovely artwork, however, wouldn't add up to much if the game was plagued by the sluggish performance that characterized most CD-ROM titles at the time.

To figure out the best way to tackle the speed issue, Vince did a little math. "I could assume that a CD-ROM could give me 150K a second at a frame rate of 15 frames per second (fps)," which was an acceptable rate for creating the illusion of movement. "That gave me 10K a frame." Allowing for sound effects, which Vince estimated would require about 2K per frame, he was eventually left with a scant 8K per frame for video. (An average full-screen color graphic occupies approximately 60K.) To hit the 10K-per-frame goal, Vince would have to use compression technology, which condenses the file for storage and then decompresses it as the program displays it on the screen.

Vince Lee at work.

Jack Sorensen, Director of Business Operations.

Vince's Lee's first "crude" experiment of the game wound up in the final version as Chapter 1— Flight Training.

First Try

With those numbers in mind, Vince began experimenting with 3-D terrains and simple animations that he created to test his design concept. Compared to the release version of Rebel Assault, Vince calls his initial mock-up "pretty crude" in look, feel, and performance. "I had this fractal landscape that was kind of a figure-eight canyon and had this animation," an X-wing that he'd drawn by hand, "flying through the figure eight, banking through turns when you moved the joystick."

When Jack Sorensen saw the experiment, he wasn't exactly bowled over. "It looked kind of ugly and pixelated and crude, and we were all scratching our heads and going 'Oh my God.' And then the level progressed, and Vince went back and redid some things to make it look better." So much better, in fact, that this early mock-up evolved into the game as the first chapter, Rookie One's flight training mission.

One possible problem the team foresaw was the performance of single-speed CD-ROMs. "Up until the last four or five months of the project," says Jack, "we weren't sure we were going to be able to ship a single-speed version. Vince wound up hitting his head a lot of times, not sure whether he could resolve a certain problem, then 20 minutes later he'd figure it out. This happened dozens of times. He'd call Microsoft and say 'Why can't I do this?,' and they'd tell him 'Well, what you're talking about, you just can't do that.'"

Engine Design

It was this sort of restriction that prompted Vince to make an important decision early in the research phase of the project. Finding that off-the-shelf compression programs did not suit his task, he set about creating his own proprietary compression technology, which would eventually become a key element in his overall "game engine"—the core software that runs Rebel Assault.

"For a good part of the first year," says Vince, "while programming the game engine, I wasn't sure it would even work. We were running off hard drives, so I could guess it would work, but we didn't have an in-house CD pressing machine. When we actually got to real CDs, we started running into all sorts of problems." He says the problems had to do primarily with the way a PC communicates with a CD-ROM drive. "With CD drives, the computer reads a block of information at a time. This might be acceptable for cut scenes [the cinematic, movie-like scenes that move the story forward between missions] but it wouldn't work with continuous 3-D animation." So he created his own data streaming and

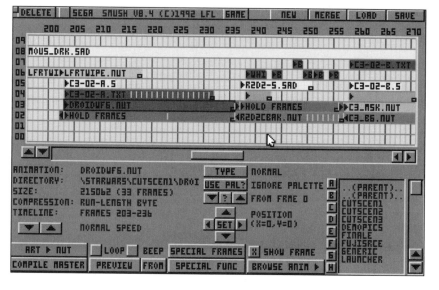

Vince Lee's interactive game design program, "SMUSH."

compression technology, which he calls SMUSH, "because it smushes everything together" into a workable size while maintaining a high level of performance and graphic resolution.

Originally created as a compression tool, the program evolved into something bigger—an interactive game design tool. Using SMUSH, with its clever timetable-like design and point-and-click interface, Vince was able to "wire together" the game's various elements, including 3-D scenery and vehicles, 2-D cut scenes, sound effects, music, and player control. "What it allows you to do is take raw animations and compress them into a format that it understands, and once everything is in that format, you can treat all the little animation blocks as entities that can be cut together. You can overlay them, move them around and, in the case of the playable levels, interact with them," which allows Vince to test each stage of the game as he develops it, on the fly.

Liftoff

Once Vince had determined, in theory anyway, that he would be able to achieve his goal—3-D flight running at a very convincing 15 frames per second—the project moved from the research phase into real development. A "ship date" goal, the date by which the company wanted the product shipped to stores, and shortly thereafter made available to the public, was set: Christmas '93. Having earned with his research the role of project leader, Vince also assumed most of the responsibility for making the proposed ship date.

What exactly does a project leader's job entail? Steve Dauterman, Director of Production, who is essentially the executive producer of all the company's titles, explains: "Project leaders have a producer role, as well as that of writer, director, and actor, even. Most project leaders come out of a programming background, though we have artists, or designer/lead artists, that become project leaders as well." As in film, the producer's first step is to put together a crew, or team. "The project leader is assigned artists and programmers to work with. In Vince's case," as far as programming was concerned, "it was mostly him, except for the installation program and some minor features, which were done by other programmers."

**Steve Dauterman,
Director of Production.**

Art was to be handled by professional designers. Therefore, the next big step was to find the talent to create and animate the game's 3-D artwork. With an estimated 600MB of space to work with, creating the artwork for Rebel Assault (as you will see) was no small affair.

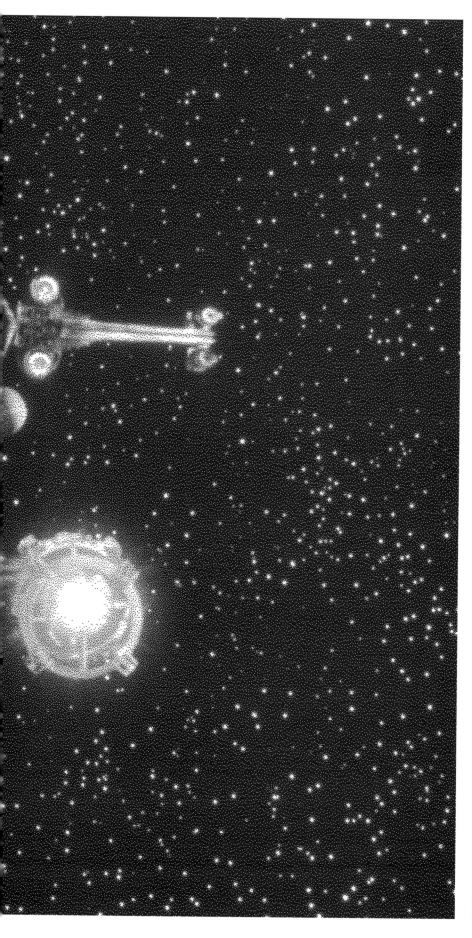

PART TWO

Lights, Cameras, Rebels in Action

THE LUCASARTS ART DEPARTMENT, a short walk across the parking lot from the main building, is a whimsical place. Inside, it is dark. Instead of the harsh overhead fluorescent lights found in most offices, the art department is illuminated by softer, warmer, incandescent floor lamps. Arty movie memorabilia, stuffed dinosaurs, and assorted toys, including squirt guns, model rocketships, and heroic action figures lay scattered everywhere, giving the place the look of a day-care center for grownups. Populating the space are creative types hunched over light tables, tracing animation cels or seated at large-screen computers working with electronic styluses on digital drawing pads, creating cartoon characters and breathtaking backgrounds for the company's entertainment titles.

Artistically Speaking

In one corner of the building sits Collette Michaud, Art Director. It was Collette to whom Vince Lee turned to find 3-D designers to work on Rebel Assault. As Art Director, it was up to Collette to build an art team for the project, compile the art and animation lists (which are similar to the production "shot lists" film studios create to track every shot that will appear in a film), estimate and track the project's art budget, and generally see to it that the artwork got done on time, according to the overall project schedule.

**A dark and mysterious place:
the art department.**

Collette Michaud, Art Director, who also inspired Commander Ru Murleen in the game.

"It took about six months to ramp-up a full production team," says Collette. "When we originally started the game, 3-D graphics were not being used in the games we developed. It was difficult finding 3-D artists who were interested in creating graphics for low-resolution games. Another difficult decision was which software and hardware platform to use." The company considered purchasing costly Silicon Graphics workstations like the ones used by Industrial Light and Magic (ILM) to create the special effects for some of Hollywood's biggest blockbusters including *Jurassic Park* and *Terminator 2*, but ultimately decided to stick with PC hardware and software. Collette adds, "We thought it would be overkill for our first 3-D project. Instead, we decided to go with Autodesk 3D Studio on the PC to create the images and animations necessary for Rebel Assault."

Digital Hollywood North

While the high-tech buzz these days centers on "Digital Hollywood"— the convergence of digital technology and Hollywood in a whole new category of cinematic entertainment titles—LucasArts has, in a sense, been creating movie games for a decade now. So rather than approach the Rebel Assault production like a film, Collette took the same tact that had worked for the company in the past. "We approached it like our other

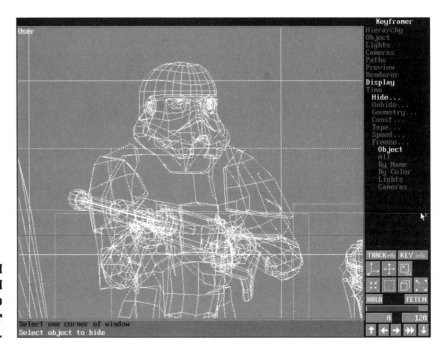

Autodesk's 3D Studio, a PC-based 3-D modeling, rendering, and animation program, was used to create the artwork for Rebel Assault.

games. The artists do everything—from design to color to animation—from start to finish. I hired artists I thought were flexible overall." Finding three "really good" 3-D artists took six months. "Each did modeling, animation, level design, wire frames [the process of building an object in 3-D—an X-wing, for example], then texture mapping, rendering, and animating. In addition to this, each artist also created backgrounds for the missions, both space and landscapes, and cut scenes as well."

Graphics and Story Are Everything

"Ron Lussier, the project's lead 3-D artist/animator, went to great pains," says Collette, "to bring to Rebel Assault dazzling graphics."

Around this time (about six months after he had started his initial design experiment) Vince Lee had worked out the overall storyline of the game. "We pretty much knew that it was going to run parallel to the *Star Wars* stories," Vince says, "…that it was going to be basically the original *Star Wars*. I had an idea what the levels were going to be and that the story kind of revolved around the levels. I thought, 'Okay, start back on Tatooine and end up destroying the Death Star'," as in the film. "It was just a matter of filling in things in between. But streaming technology

Ron Lussier,
lead 3-D artist/
animator.

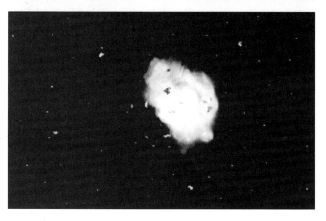

Vince Lee's original thumbnail
storyboard sketches.

Vince Lee: "I thought…'Start back
on Tatooine…

…and end up
destroying the
Death Star'."

15

Rebel Assault team members watched the *Star Wars* trilogy many times to study the look and feel of flying ships.

(in SMUSH) only lends itself to certain kinds of levels, like flying down a canyon or flying through asteroids. So I sat down with the artists and said 'This is what we can do: fly in a cave, fly in an asteroid field…'"

Galactic Inspiration

Vince and the artists say they watched the *Star Wars* films many times for inspiration—to reacquaint themselves with the story, to find scenes that could be used as cut scenes in the game, and to study the "look and feel" of the various ships flying through space and over land.

Once they had an overall sense of what the game's levels, or missions, were, it was time to start creating the artwork. The artwork in Rebel Assault is divided into two main categories—missions and cut scenes. Exactly how does an artist go about creating missions and cut scenes?

3-D Model Building

For starters, Ron Lussier set about creating the primary vehicles for the title, since they would be required for nearly every mission and cut scene. This, says Collette, was probably the single most time-consuming process.

Ron Lussier at his PC workstation. (Notice the *Return of the Jedi* backdrop, a souvenir from the film.)

To recreate vehicles for the game, Ron studied the *Star Wars* trio of sketchbooks, hobby model kits, and Lucasfilm's archived sketches and models, including:

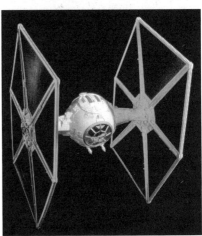

A TIE fighter model from *Star Wars*.

A TIE fighter sketch from *Star Wars*.

Ron studied existing artwork and models collected from several sources, including a series of exceedingly detailed *Star Wars* sketchbooks, off-the-shelf *Star Wars* hobby model kits, and the nearby Lucasfilm headquarters where the actual vehicle models used in the *Star Wars* films are housed. Among those models is a large-scale X-wing model, whose dimensions Ron copied down part by part. Ron used 3D Studio to draw 3-D digital versions of the *Star Wars* vehicles that were true to the originals.

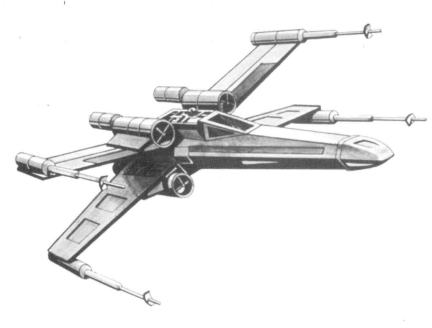

An X-wing sketch from *The Empire Strikes Back*.

An X-wing model from *Star Wars*.

WALKER 1·28·79

A sketch of an All Terrain Scout Transport (AT-ST) with an All Terrain Armored Transport (AT-AT), or "walker," in the background...

...and a sketch of an All Terrain Personal Transport (AT-PT), both from *The Empire Strikes Back.*

3-D Wire-Frame Art

The process of creating 3-D models is a slow, painstaking one. The first step is to create a wire frame, which is a collection of points that the artist connects to one another with lines, or "wires," to create shapes, or polygons, that, when strung together, look like a see-through, 3-D model. To create the 3-D wire-frame model based on its points and lines, however, the computer must calculate all of the vehicle's described connections, which can range from a few to a few thousand, by performing a process called rendering. Rendering 3-D graphics like this takes anywhere from 2 minutes to 20 or more hours to complete and requires 100% of the processing power of the artist's machine. For this reason, Ron often had to shuttle between LucasArts and his home, where he had another computer system, alternately using one computer to design and the other to render.

Using an electronic drawing tablet and stylus as his digital paper and pen, Ron creates a 3-D, X-wing wire-frame model from basic 2-D shapes. The process is a slow and painstaking one.

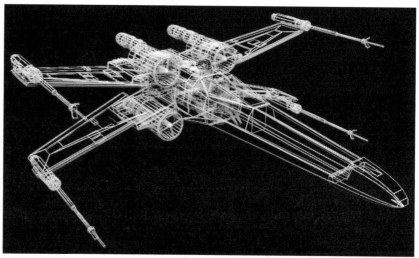

Ron's X-wing wire-frame model up close.

A TIE interceptor wire-frame.

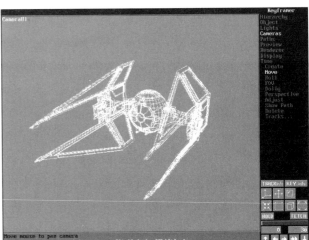

A sketch of the same vehicle from *Return of the Jedi*.

Texture Mapping

Once the 3-D wire-frame model is created, the ship's overall shape and dimensions can be evaluated and refined. It can be turned this way and that in 3-D space, but the model does not yet look real. To give the model a tangible, filled-in look, the artist next applies a texture map to the surfaces of the wire-frame model—the digital equivalent of giving the model a paint job. First, the artist designates which surfaces are solid (or opaque), like panels and engines, and which surfaces are transparent, like the cockpit windscreen. A color texture map, which is either hand-drawn pixel by pixel or created by combining preexisting patterns, is then applied to the ship's solid surfaces, giving the model a clean, flat, metallic look and feel.

For the final touch, Ron dirties the model to add a truer sense of surface reality.

Collette explains, "One of the things Ron developed in the R & D process was a way to make the models look beat-up and dirty. 3-D graphics typically are very clean looking, so it was a challenge to make the models appear like the ships in the movie."

After Ron created digital models of most of the fighters, he set about building the first levels of the game. During the first third of the project, he was, for the most part, on his own; two artists who had done some early work on the project eventually left the company. One of the artists, Dan Colon, did a lot of work creating levels 3 and 8 before he left. He also built the walker and Star Destroyer. So Collette set about searching for two additional 3-D artist/animators to join the Rebel Assault art team.

To give the wire-frame model a filled-in look, the artist applies texture maps to its surfaces.

For the final touch, the artist "dirties" the model with custom textures for a more realistic-looking final product.

3-D artist/animator Dan Colon
was the sole creator behind Rebel
Assault's breathtaking Imperial
walker level.

Dan studied actual sketches and illustrations from *The Empire Strikes Back.*

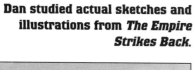

Chapter 8 gives players a
Luke Skywalker perspective on
the Imperial walkers.

Creating a Level

Creating a level, says Ron, goes something like this: "I had some initial storyboards that were somewhat loose, so I'd try to rework them when I started into a level, figure out how to interpret the storyboards into an actual playing session, figuring how to fly through the level, attack and shoot at these targets, and fly through space. Some, like the snow caves, which did a lot of branching, I would draw up." To visualize this sort of complexity, Ron creates a map of the entire level, showing each branch and the course it takes the player through.

Ron's next step entails turning his one-dimensional map into a virtual landscape or spacescape, depending on the mission scenario. "Using the map as an overhead, I bring it into 3D Studio, into what's called Shaper, a 2-D creation tool for laying the map out. Initially, I used those paths to extrude cylinders, but I eventually figured out that that wouldn't work, so I used two halves instead, so you're within these bowls, flying."

Making the Grade

To give the landscapes a realistic-looking elevation and surface texture, Ron uses the shareware program GIF2DXF. "You draw a GIF image in black and white, where black is the lowest elevation and white is the highest and gray represents the elevations in between. Then you cut a black trench and soften the edges as you go up the elevation with lighter gray or white. Then you create a .dxf file out of those height values,"

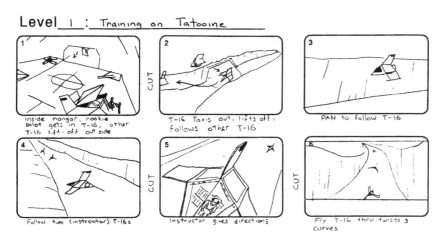

Ron referred to Vince Lee's thumbnail storyboard sketches as a guide to create mission levels.

The final effect appears graduated in color and texture, and realistic looking.

which the program calculates based on those drawn-in shades. A .dxf file, explains Ron, is a standard digital exchange format for describing a file that contains 3-D geometry.

Once the landscape or spacescape is built, he has a course laid out that he can turn into an animated mission by flying his 3-D vehicles through it, using 3D Studio's animation tools.

Using 3D Studio, the artist chooses a camera angle with which to "shoot" an animation scene, then designates key frames along the course the player will fly.

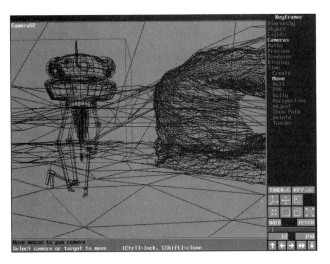

In this scene from *The Empire Strikes Back*, a probe droid homes-in on Chewbacca.

A probe droid (or "probot") sketch from the film *The Empire Strikes Back*.

Sequences from the rendered probe droid cut scene.

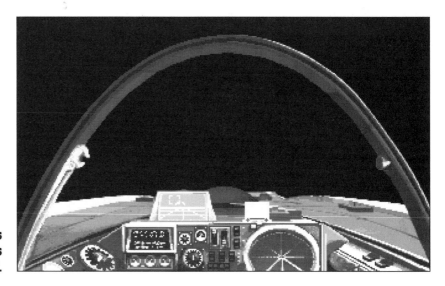

Cockpit interiors, such as this A-wing's, were added to levels after they were completed.

"You run the camera path through that," says Ron, "which is really all a lot of this was—flying a camera through a situation then putting a still image of the cockpit on top of that." As in traditional filmmaking, the artist can adjust certain camera parameters, including focal length, to control how a scene is shot.

The artist, now playing the role of both digital director and cinematographer, may choose to light a scene from an overhead angle, as though it were high noon, or from behind the player's ship, creating the long shadows of sunset. For the camera angle, the artist can shoot from within the cockpit, as in the in-your-face asteroid missions, or from behind the ship, tailing it, as in the first mission in which Rookie One learns to fly.

For example, the dogfight sequence in the Rebel Assault introduction was originally described as "X-wings and TIE fighters dogfighting over a Star Destroyer." Ron took this simple description and choreographed, animated, shot, lit, and edited it into one of the most exciting scenes in the game.

Animation

To direct the actual motion—the animation that the camera will record—the artist designates certain key frames, or milestones, along the course the player will fly. For simple shots, like the first straight-away trench in

Beggar's Canyon, the artist has only to indicate a few key frames—from the very beginning of the mission to, say, the frame just before Rookie One executes his or her first right-hand turn—and then let the 3D Studio software automatically calculate the frames in between, smoothly and convincingly. This timesaving technique is called interpolation. For fast-moving, shifting points in the course (a turn, for example) the artist must indicate substantially more key frames, spaced closer together, so that the software interpolates the frames between the key frames with greater smoothness and detail.

Final Rendering

When these parameters are set, the artist renders the entire scene, in much the same way the vehicles were originally rendered, but this time, instead of processing a single, static object, the computer must calculate a moving, three-dimensional environment, complete with lighting and camera effects. The result is a self-contained, animated flying sequence that lacks any sensation of player control or targeting. (Those elements are added to the sequences using SMUSH, as described below.)

Eventually, Collette found the two additional 3-D artist/animators she needed—David Vallone and Richard Green—who would create

Rounding out the Rebel Assault 3-D art team were artists Richard Green...

...whose first assignment was Chapter 5...

...and David Vallone...

...who jumped in to finish Chapter 8.

missions and cut scenes under Ron's direction. In addition, she assigned Aaron Muszalski the role of lead art technician. Aaron's primary responsibilities were to capture from the *Star Wars* films the video footage used to create the game's many cinematic cut scenes and to compress the artist/animators' individual missions into the frame size that Vince had established.

Richard Green, who came on board with some computer graphics experience, says the process of creating missions was pleasantly flexible. "I came in two-thirds through the project. The game was broken down into easy-to-assign levels. The ships all existed, and when I came in Ron was at Level 4, so I got the next level on the hit list." In the beginning, Richard says, he spent time "learning how they wanted the artwork to look, the pacing of things. It wasn't really a fixed structure. You'd do the intro, the gameplay, the outro"—his word for the wrap-up scene that runs after the player completes a level.

David Vallone had similar thoughts: "I started in the middle of the project. Everything was pretty much set, and I was given Level 8, with

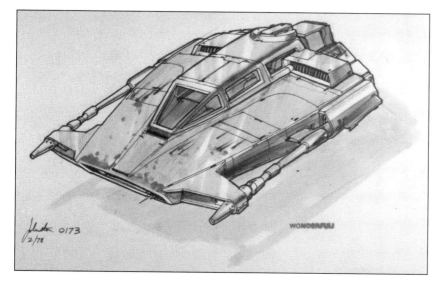

The artists' objects of affection:

A snowspeeder illustration from *The Empire Strikes Back.*

Also from *Empire*: an illuminated Hoth background.

An illustration by Ralph McQuarrie of Luke's snowspeeder crash.

the snowspeeder. I did the cut scenes for that. The biggest level I did was Level 11, the Yavin Planet, which I designed as I went along. There wasn't a set idea of how this level should be. We were given lots of creative freedom to time it, pace it. A lot of it was Vince's idea, originally, but we were constantly adding and changing and developing."

A Y-wing trailed by
a trio of X-wings.

Two Imperial
Star Destroyers
orbiting Hoth.

A high-detail Star Destroyer model.

And from *Star Wars*, an X-wing
en route to Tatooine.

Improvising On-the-Fly

As lead 3-D artist/animator, Ron oversaw the overall look and feel of Rebel Assault's mission artwork and animation. "I would clarify cut scenes, screen direction, continuity. I did a decent amount of that, yet tried to let the guys go on their own on their levels."

Richard adds that sometimes "it was almost like you didn't need a storyboard. We'd say, 'Okay, two X-wings have to fly in this shot,' and then you'd choreograph it however you wanted."

"Right," agrees David. They asked themselves, "What is the most dramatic and interesting way that two X-wings can fly through a scene? Whatever it was that you had to do, and that was what sort of kept it interesting—that you did get to make up a lot of it as you went along. Going through and laying out sequences and previewing, testing, before the final render. You'd test for action, and if it was too long or too short, you could make adjustments sometimes." Collette estimates that each level took approximately one-and-a-half to two months to complete.

Because the game was being made for CD-ROM, the art team says, the length of a given level was never really much of an issue. Still, there

A frame from *Star Wars*...

...and from *The Empire Strikes Back*...

...both of which appear as cut
scenes in Rebel Assault.

were some issues of length to consider. Initially, Vince says, "I counted
out 20 levels, smaller ones, but after we started working on it, it was
taking so long to get animation done on each level that we decided it was
better to do fewer levels and make them longer." A similar decision was
made for the cinematic cut scene sequences. "Originally, we had very simple
cut scenes—one or two for entry, exit. Mostly the levels were done in
sequence," he says, and as they progressed, the "cut scenes got more and
more elaborate." Which leads to the other half of the art department's big
contribution to Rebel Assault—cut scenes.

"Shooting" Cut Scenes

"Basically," says Collette, "they were created from the initial storyboards
that Vince laid out. Because we were working on CD-ROM, there was

no limit to the number of frames in the cut scenes. Ron, Rich and Dave would come up with these incredible cut scenes that would constantly amaze me. Aaron was responsible for all of the video-captured scenes from the film. A lot of times when we'd pull a cut scene out of a film it included a moving background. Aaron would have to pull out the characters and very carefully cut around each character's animation and put them onto a static background."

One example of this technique can be seen during Rebel Assault's opening sequence in the scene where Luke Skywalker walks toward the two setting suns and stops to gaze across the arid, salmon-hued, Tatooine horizon. Another clever trick occurs at the end of the game when Rookie One receives an award for successfully destroying the Empire's Death Star. The footage for this scene of Rookie One ambling up to the front stage was taken directly from the award ceremony scene at the end of *Star Wars*.

Aaron explains how the footage was altered to suit Rebel Assault: "In the film, Han, Luke, and Chewbacca get the award. But you're not playing with them in Rebel Assault, so we had to fix that. I extracted the characters and painted out Han and the Wookiee, but because they were overlapping Luke's shoulder, he had to recreate the missing shoulder and arm from other bits."

Aaron Muszalski, lead art technician, was responsible for all the video-captured cut scenes.

Here Aaron "cut around" Luke Skywalker's character and recast it onto a static background.

For the awards ceremony scene at the end of the game Aaron carefully "cut" Chewie and Han Solo from the original footage...

...to create Rookie One's amble to glory.

Face to Face

Cut scenes that were not taken directly from the films, Ron says, were modeled by the artists and rendered in 3-D. The 2-D characters like Rookie One's colleagues and Darth Vader's henchman—The Commander—were, in fact, inspired by LucasArts employees.

These 2-D characters were created by artist/animators Bill Tiller and Leonard Robel. By capturing several video frames of each face uttering a few phrases, the artists essentially created a digital-clip library from which they could draw to animate the character's dialog. The speech was recorded later, near the end of the project, when all of the cut scenes were finished.

Bill Tiller and Leonard Robel created and animated 2-D characters inspired by LucasArts employees.

Artist Mike Levine provided special video assistance for Rebel Assault.

The cast of employees who inspired the characters includes:

Associate Producer Wayne Cline, who also helped test the game...

...was a Rebel Soldier model (with artist Steve Purcell looking over his shoulder).

Director of Business Operations Jack Sorensen...

...inspired the Lt. Turland Hack character.

Artist Sean Turner rendered as the evil Empire Commander...

...opposite his Hollywood counterpart, Peter Cushing.

Artist Jon Knoles, who also helped with additional art, including creating vehicle cockpits...

...modeled as the Rookie Thurlow Harris character.

And artist Peter Chan...

...inspired the Capt. Merrick Simms character.

All pilots were modeled after the 'real' Rebel pilots from the films, like Wedge Antilles from *The Empire Strikes Back*.

Compression

"SMUSH supports a variety of different compression methods," Vince explains. "The one used for any particular scene depends on the nature of the imagery and the amount of on-screen movement. The most interesting one is used to compress scenes where there is complex full-screen movement. It analyzes each frame of an animation and tries to reduce that image to its rudimentary elements. The image is later reconstructed from these elements when the SMUSHed animation is played back from a CD drive."

This compression method, however, works best with certain types of imagery and underwent improvements during development. Ron relates the art team's experience with the earliest compression method: "Initially, [we compressed some animations] and we said 'Oh my God, my art's getting ruined!'" This was unacceptable, so the team did some experimenting. Ron used different texture maps, finding ones that compressed well, while Vince worked to improve the compression algorithm. In the end, they came up with imagery and a version of SMUSH that was able to keep textures and edge detail that were lost in the early tests.

Once the artist/animators were satisfied with their missions, they turned them over to Aaron for compression. "I compressed all the artwork to 256 colors" for the PC version, says Aaron, "then I compressed it again for the Sega CD version." Because the Sega CD allows two layers of 16-color graphics, Aaron compressed those missions twice, creating a total of 32 colors for the Sega CD version. The Macintosh version of the game, which supports 256 colors, uses the same graphics as the PC version.

How did the artists react to seeing artwork that they might have created in more than 1000 colors altered so drastically? Aaron says, "I don't think I won any friends among these guys." But there were no hard feelings, says Richard Green. "He helped a lot of shots—improved them. The Level 2 death scene was much better because he was able to produce the colors just right."

Despite Aaron's required compression of their original artwork, which reduces color and resolution, the artists were pleased with the results, as in this hot Chapter 2 death scene.

Piece by Piece

After he received the compressed artwork from Aaron, Vince used SMUSH to incorporate the new artwork into the ever-evolving game. Using SMUSH, Vince added to the artwork gaming elements like the enemy lasers that fire at the player and targets like TIE fighters. He also specified the level of precision with which the player must lock-on to the fighters with his or her gun sight in order to take them out. To make Vince's job of filling in targets a little less tedious, the artists created batches of ready-made targets that he could draw on and paste in as needed. "We came up with a bunch of renderings of different paths of ships coming at you—TIE fighters, for example. In any space where Vince wanted to

After he received the compressed artwork from Aaron, Vince Lee used SMUSH...

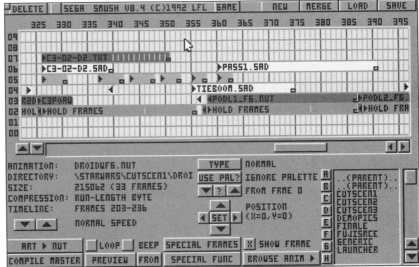

...to incorporate the artwork into the ever-evolving game...

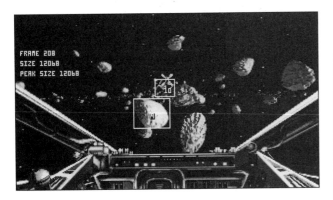

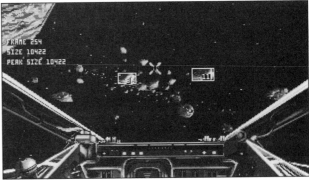

...to add gaming elements such as target details to these two asteroid levels.

Besides increasing the challenge of the game, adding extra **TIE** fighters in this sequence also provides players a greater sense of actual flight and location, relative to the Imperial Destroyers they are circling.

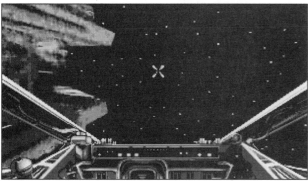

adjust the difficulty, he could just add TIE fighters, like when you pass the first Star Destroyer." In addition to adding greater challenge to playing the level, the TIE fighters, says Aaron, serve a second, perhaps more subtle, purpose.

Film versus Rebel Assault

"In the movies, you cheat on a lot of shots. Like when they filmed *Star Wars*, they didn't actually have the battle going on with all those ships actually moving in 3-D space. Editing just makes it look that way; they were cut together. But these [scenes from Rebel Assault] are actual 3-D locations with consistent scale. That's why adding TIE fighters helps." It gives players a sense of place (theirs) relative to the Imperial Star Destroyers around which they are soaring.

The process of creating the Rebel Assault artwork continued, for the most part, in a routine manner—level after level, cut scene after cut scene. With the Christmas ship date coming up fast (it was by now the summer of '93), the art department, along with everyone else involved in the project, was beginning to wonder whether they would make the date.

The Deadline Looms...

Although the team was making impressive progress, there was still much work to be done before Rebel Assault could premiere on players' computer screens. Many pieces of the puzzle still needed to come together, including recording the spoken lines of dialog, adapting John Williams's London Symphony Orchestra *Star Wars* soundtrack, creating sound effects, ramping up a marketing and promotion campaign, producing a demo version of the product for software retailers to run in their stores, and, most important of all, testing the game to make sure that not only did it play without crashing but that it played in a manner that was engaging, exciting, and, above all, fun.

But fun was hardly the word anyone would choose to describe the collective Rebel Assault frame of mind that summer. The project had reached full steam and was rounding the final bend into the grueling final stretch known simply as "The Crunch."

Get a first-person perspective on stormtroopers in LucasArts's Dark Forces game, coming Winter 1994.

Listen up, Rookie One. You're in for some heavy flying and fighting. Here's a little secret that will make it easier for you to survive the grueling levels that follow. By performing the "secret cheat code" below, you'll arm yourself with the power to instantly erase damage points and return your health to 100%; to skip past mission sequences and cut scenes; and, for Mac and PC pilots, to jump instantly to any level in the game with a single keystroke.

PC & Sega CD Pilots

At the beginning of the game, when the animated LucasArts logo first appears, perform the following sequence with the joystick (or gamepad) and fire button:

PC			Sega CD		
Joystick		**Button**	**Joystick**		**Button**
Up	+	Fire	Up	+	A
Down	+	Fire	Down	+	A
Left	+	Fire	Up	+	A
Right	+	Fire	Up	+	A
			Left	+	A
			Right	+	A

You'll hear a jingle sound and then a chorus of voices sings the word "LucasArts," indicating that the cheat mode is enabled. Once you're playing the game, the following cheat keys are active:

PC & Macintosh Pilots

[+] on the numeric keypad erases damage and restores health to 100%.

[Esc] skips to the next mission sequence or cut scene.

On the Main Keyboard:
[1] jumps to Chapter 1
[2] jumps to Chapter 2
...and so on, up to...
[9] jumps to Chapter 9
[A] jumps to Chapter 10
[B] jumps to Chapter 11
...and so on, up to...
[F] jumps to Chapter 15

Macintosh Pilots

To activate the Mac's secret level, perform the following: Choose Game Options from the Star Wars Rebel Assault main menu. Hold down the [⌘], [Option], [Control], and [Shift] keys. Move the arrow cursor to the space between the Rapid Fire and Shut Down Other Applications buttons, then click the mouse (or the fire button on your joystick) three times quickly.

A new button, Yoda's Power Mode, will appear. Now you can use the PC and Macintosh pilots cheat keys listed below. A single click on Yoda's Power Mode toggles the mode on or off.

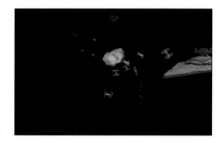

Sega CD Pilots

[C] skips to the next mission sequence or cut scene.

Start pauses the game and lists the Rebel Assault menu, from which you can select Restore Health, then press [A], then Start to return to the game with health restored to 100%.

Macintosh/Sega CD Passwords

Chapter	Easy	Normal	Hard
2	bossk	bothan	bordok
3	engret	herglic	skynx
4	ralrra	leeni	defel
5	frija	thrawn	jedgar
6	lafra	lwyll	madine
7	derlin	mazzic	tarkin
8	moltok	julpa	mothma
9	morag	morrt	glayyd
10	tantiss	muftak	ottega
11	oswafl	raskar	rishii
12	klaaty	jhoff	izrina
13	irenez	ithor	karrde
14	lianna	umwak	vonzel
15	pakka	orlok	ossus
End	norval	nkllon	malani

PC Passwords

Chapter	Easy	Normal	Hard
4	falcon	biggs	ackbar
7	anoat	kaiburr	fornax
11	yuzzem	mynock	bespin
15	brigia	dagobah	kessel
End	greedo	mimban	organa

Good luck, Rookie One—and "May the Force be with you..."

Chapter 1
Flight Training

It is morning at a Rebel Base on planet Tatooine, where a young pilot is embarking on a crucial training flight.

Officer Hack: "You shouldn't have any problems—Beggar's Canyon isn't half as tough as the runs we used to do. Good luck!"

Green Leader: "We're approaching the canyon run."

Green Leader: "Prepare to engage target drones. Shoot any we pass over, but stay with us!"

TIP   This level is tough, Rookie One. Be gentle and subtle on the joystick, using light taps—don't overcompensate. Also, take the right turn here and follow Simms—it's easier than going left, despite his warning.

TIP   Don't stray too far off course—most targets will drift directly in your path, making them easy to hit.

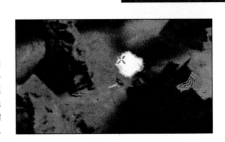

TIP   To complete this mission you must hit five or more target drones, or else Simms will make you play again.

Chapter 2
Asteroid Field Training

Commander Jake Farrell only SOUNDS grumpy.

Be polite and you'll get along fine.

Cmdr. Farrell: "Shoot the ice asteroids, but dodge the rocky ones…"

TIP Hit ice asteroids directly in your path and skip those too far off course. Keep your laser crosshair as far away as possible from rocky asteroids, or else you'll collide with them and receive damage.

See—he really IS an okay guy.

Chapter 3
Planet Kolaador

Cmdr. Murleen: "You impressed Commander Farrell…That's not easy. Me, I'm a little more forgiving, but the course ahead isn't…"

The planet Kolaador's crystaline rock formations offer the perfect playground for Rookies in training.

Cmdr. Murleen: "…so follow me closely, and May the Force be with you."

TIP This lesson is tough on purpose, to see if you're ready to take on the Empire. Now more than ever, a subtle wrist will save you. Except for a few ups and downs, the course is mostly straight—stay low, and concentrate on following Ru's maneuvers as closely as possible.

TIP For PC Pilots: Here's where you earn your first password.

Cmdr. Murleen: "Follow me to base and we'll get you assigned to a squadron. And while we're waiting, I'll let you buy me a drink for that fancy flying."

Chapter 4
Star Destroyer Attack

The Empire in hot pursuit of a Rebel ship.

Darth Vader, Dark Lord of the Sith, is eager to crush the Rebels.

R2-D2 and C-3PO have plans of their own—they're not sticking around for this round.

Back on Kolaador: "Attention all pilots: Report to battle stations immediately. Tatooine Base is under attack!"

TIP A steady hand will assure you a lock with your torpedo. If you misfire, Cmdr. Murleen will take a shot after you...and toss a little scorn your way, as well.

TIP Patience and accuracy are the key here. You must knock out all of the Star Destroyer's gun targets...

TIP ...and the domes on top in order to get a chance to launch your torpedo.

Chapter 5
Tatooine Attack

The Rebel pilots race to Tatooine Base...

Officer Hack: "Mayday! We are under attack!" But the Rebels are too late, and the Empire scores a devastating hit against the Rebel Base.

TIP The trick here, Rookie One, is to start firing IMMEDIATELY when the mission begins.

Take out all three TIEs immediately and you won't have to chase any strays on the treacherous course ahead. Miss any of them, and you'll start all over again.

Cmdr. Murleen gives the order: Take out the trio of TIEs.

Cmdr. Simms and Rookie Harris recruit you for a side mission, while Murleen takes a temporary leave.

TIP Blast as many ground targets as possible for bonus points. Don't worry, they won't shoot back—but be careful not to shoot your fellow Rebel pilots by accident!

Chapter 6
Asteroid Field Chase

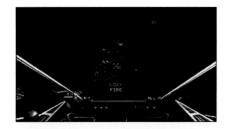

TIP Focus only on those ice asteroids in your direct path, while avoiding rocky asteroids.

TIP Shoot ice asteroids while they are far away, and the explosion will often destroy nearby ice asteroids.

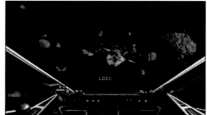

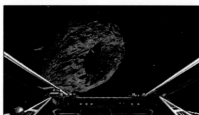

You'll squeeze through this donut asteroid without a hitch, Rookie One...

...but that **TIE** on your tail won't be as lucky.

PC Pilots leave this level with another password.

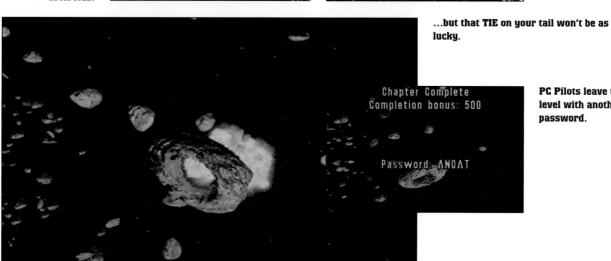

Chapter 7
Imperial Probe Droids

TIP The quickest way through the droid cave is to take the split-offs in this order:

Left...

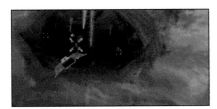

Left...

Right...

On the remote ice planet Hoth, an unexpected visitor drops in.

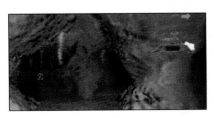

Left...

Left.

Chapter 8
Imperial Walkers

Snowspeeder pilot: "Rookie One, good to have you on board. Let's get this over with."

TIP   The Walker's lasers aren't particularly damaging.

Snowspeeder pilot: "I'm locking in your navigation computer. Arm your assault guns. Now follow me."

TIP   As you hit the Walker's panels they turn from light beige to dark gray. You must knock out almost all of the Walker's beige panels to complete the mission.

TIP   When the Choose Attack light flashes, you may pick one of two attack routes to fly...

TIP   For route A, point your joystick left and press button B, for route B, point right and press button B.

TIP   Get too close to the Walker on passes between its legs and you'll suffer ship damage. Steer close enough to hit, but not too close that you scrape its legs.

Chapter 9
Stormtroopers

After a safe Snowspeeder crash landing, Rookie One is left alone on the Stormtrooper-infested planet.

TIP Lucky for you, Rookie One, the Stormtroopers aren't all that bright. Spray your laser back and forth to take them down quickly.

TIP The "correct" path in this mission is random. To figure out which route to choose, go either left or right at the first split.

TIP If your initial path leads you into a Stormtrooper ambush, you'll be sent back to the beginning. This time, choose the other direction. That is, if you chose left and were ambushed, go right this time.

TIP If you aren't ambushed after the first split, keep choosing the same direction for all of the remaining splits. For example: If you go right and are not ambushed, keep choosing the right fork at every split thereafter.

Finally—a breakthrough!

A safe getaway, just in the nick of time.

Chapter 10
Protect Rebel Transport

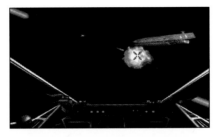

TIP Don't worry about hitting the transport pod—your lasers won't do it any damage.

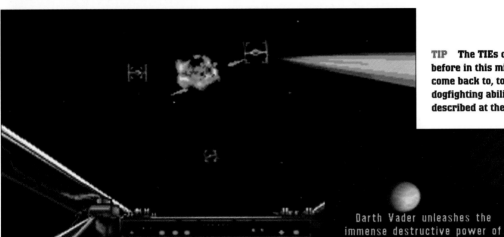

TIP The TIEs come on stronger than before in this mission—it's a good one to come back to, to brush up on your dogfighting abilities, using the cheat described at the beginning.

In his continuing quest to locate the Rebels...

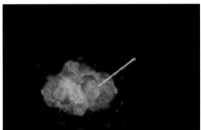

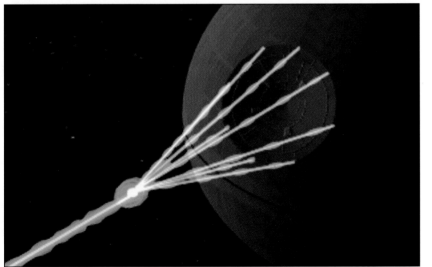

Imperial Commander: "The target has been destroyed, sir. What is our new heading?"

TIP PC Pilots: Congratulations, Rookie One—your third password.

Chapter 11
Yavin Training

Yavin Tactician: "An analysis of the plans provided by Princess Leia has demonstrated a weakness in the Battle Station. The target area is only two meters wide. Only a precise hit will set up a chain reaction that should destroy the station."

Yavin Tactician: "The Death Star will enter this system within three hours. To prepare for its arrival, we will run a series of training exercises."

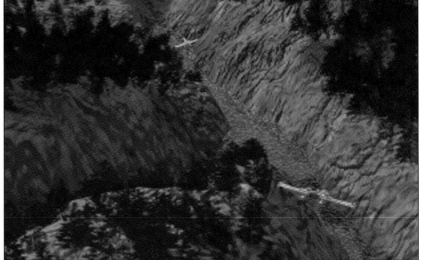

TIP   Concentrate on technique here, Rookie One, rather than shooting...

TIP   ...but make sure you take out a few targets, or else Simms will send you back for another round.

Capt. Simms: "You heard 'em. Let's do it for real, now...Launch!"

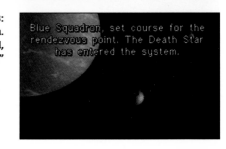

Chapter 12
Tie Attack

Capt. Simms: "We're starting our approach."

Capt. Simms: "Stay tight. Here they come!"

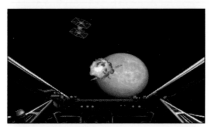

TIP When you hear Simms call out for help, make sure you nail this trio of TIEs, or else...

TIP You must save Simms in order to complete this level and continue.

Chapter 13
Death Star Surface

Capt. Simms: "Blue Two, start your approach. Accelerate to attack speed."

Cmdr. Ru Murleen: "Okay, we can do this. Just keep your eyes open."

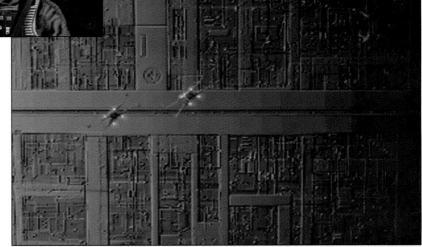

TIP   Stay low to avoid getting hit by ground lasers.

TIP   Cut back and forth swiftly to rain fire on ground targets

TIP   For a greater hit rate and score, venture higher on the screen—after you have enough experience and can anticipate where targets are and when they fire.

Chapter 14
Surface Cannon

Ru Murleen: "Okay, let's go in..."

TIP   Blast the blue panels in as few passes as possible...

...so that you'll have fewer TIEs to contend with.

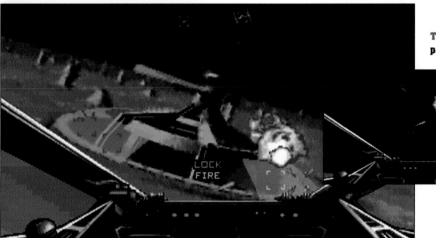

TIP   **PC Pilots:** Complete this level to earn your fourth password.

TIP   Try to keep a steady hand here Rookie One, and line up your lasers so that they follow the arc of the turn, taking out the targets as you circle.

Chapter 15
Death Star Trench

TIP In the first round, try to shoot canons in the distance, before you get close enough for them to shoot you.

Simms takes his shot at the exhaust port...and misses. The Rebel Alliance is counting on you, Rookie One!

TIP Try to knock out all five blue shields to avoid damage to your ship as you pass through them.

It's up to you, kid.

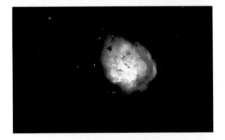

TIP Steady, Rookie One...line up the sight and fire when it locks on target. Now!

Rookie One: "It's away..."

Rookie One: "Yahoo!"

You have defeated me...
...this time.

Congratulations, Rookie One!

FUTURE SHOCK

The Crunch

IT WAS BY NOW THE SUMMER OF '93. The much hoped-for pre-Christmas ship date was less than five months away. Until now, the two busiest groups had been the artists and Vince Lee and a few of his helper programmers, but it was time for more people to get involved in the Rebel Assault project in a big way.

As completed missions rolled in from the art department, Vince had his hands full with the programming alone. And on top of that, there was a long list of tasks to be done, including writing a manual, creating a data card, casting voice talent to record the game's spoken dialog, adding sound effects and music, and the task that would prove especially involving for Vince and company, initiating the quality assurance process (referred to simply as Q/A).

Pressure Cooker

Steve Dauterman describes the atmosphere at the time. "The biggest nightmare was project management. In the beginning we didn't know what we were doing; we had nothing to compare it to." As they came into the final stretch, Steve says, the team asked itself, "What are we going to do to get this thing out before Christmas '93?" By this time the project had a high profile within the company, and management was willing to provide extra resources to help the team make that ship date. "Rendering

FM Towns version programmer Paul LeFevre, programmer Justin Graham, and Vince Lee.

Additional programming assistance was provided by Gary Brubaker, Mark Haigh-Hutchinson, and Aric Wilmunder.

time [for the remaining levels] was taking too long—overnight some-times—so we upgraded the artists to faster and faster machines. As faster machines became available, we could throw more machines at the artists."

On the programming side, there were challenges that had more to do with human processing power than computing power. Because Vince was being pulled in so many directions, Steve says, "a big issue was getting him to focus on game play, smoothness, and joystick control."

A prop from the film *Return of the Jedi* adorns the door leading to the 3-D artists' workspace.

Additional art assistance was
provided by art technician
Gwen Musengwa...

...artist Larry Ahern...

...and 3-D artist Ralph Gerth.

The Q/A Process

These issues, and many more, arose when the product was sent to the Q/A testing group, headed by Mark Cartwright.

"In general," Mark says, "they try to get into testing as soon as they can in order to allow the largest window of time to look at the game." In the case of Rebel Assault, Mark's team started testing the game relatively early in the process. "We started looking at Rebel Assault as soon as it

Q/A manager Mark Cartwright.

was playable, as soon as you could sit down and go through one or two levels and start to get a feel for what it was about."

In the early stages of development, he says, testing can be a complex process. "There's a lot that's not in the game yet, so the testers are constantly balancing what's there with what's going to eventually be in the game. They have to ask themselves, 'Can I really comment when it's not implemented yet?' Almost any feature can be either partially in or not in at all." Missing from Rebel Assault in the early test phase were sound effects and music, levels or parts of levels, cut scenes, and death scenes, the cinematic crashes that appear when you get wiped out in a level. "It's amazing how some seemingly unimportant features really fill a game out. You say, 'This is not very good.' Then a few weeks or a month later when you're coming to the end, you have a final version that looks good, and you're surprised. Early on, it's kind of tricky to keep in mind what's there and what's not."

Testing, 1...2...3...

What exactly does a tester test for? Mark explains: "It varies from game to game. With Rebel Assault, it was basically three things. First, straight game play and checking for bugs. 'Does it crash here?' Or, 'There's an ugly graphics glitch that happens here.' So the tester recreates it and presents the information to programming. Second, there's the whole compatibility thing. Rebel Assault caused us to create another department in Q/A. In the new department, technical specialists go through all the sound cards, CD-ROMs, and everything they can get a hold of in the market or in development and coming to market to make sure the hardware works with the game. And third, testers spend a lot of time tweaking the difficulty of game play—the challenge. A lot of action games offer easy, medium, and hard settings, so a couple of testers have to sit around and make sure that all the levels in easy are actually easy, medium are medium, and hard are hard."

With a tablet as a log book, testers kept track of bugs and suggestions as they played the game. They then forwarded that information to Vince Lee. Ultimately, says Mark, "Vince had the final say as to whether or not the suggestions were implemented in the game."

A Good Play?

Brett Tosti, one of the lead playtesters on Rebel Assault, says the relationship between Q/A and Vince was an amiable one. "Vince was very willing to delegate responsibility, and he was open to suggestions of all

Q/A tester Brett Tosti concentrated on playability and helped influence the game's final design.

sorts. In my opinion, he's one of the best programmers around. I would say 'Here is the problem,' and his response would be 'Okay, I know what it is; here, try this,' which to me is the sign of programming genius. He is very good at what he does."

Brett says he started testing Rebel Assault when it was 75 percent complete. "My first impression was, 'this looks cool, but there's not a lot of game play to it.' There would be an asteroid field, for example, and you'd be going through it, but what was I doing? Shooting things? Dodging things? It wasn't clear what was hitting you. In the TIE Attack levels, initially, only TIEs would come in, and if you missed them they would hit you. They were shooting lasers, but it was only art." So, based on his suggestions and those of his fellow Q/A testers, "they changed them from art to true lasers that could do damage to you."

Easy, Normal, Hard

Brett says he spent a lot of time concentrating on the game's overall feel, constantly evaluating whether the controls felt "right"—whether they responded properly. Initially, he says the game was "very difficult up front, and you did not get a sense of flight." He says it was as though the team had focused on making a visually pleasing program and added game play as an afterthought. Brett's other responsibility was to evaluate the game's difficulty levels. He used a software patch (a programming "fix") supplied

by Vince to adjust the difficulty—easy, medium, and hard—of each level so that the settings were true. "I would say, 'That's too much damage,' or 'This target is too easy or too hard to hit on this level,' so I had to adjust the game to what I thought was proper." Another adjustment Brett suggested that made it into the final product was the ability to choose the frame rate at which the game plays. "On a fast machine, you get a very fast game, and this is great, but sometimes it's too fast!"

An avid game player whose video gaming experience dates back to Pong, Brett says putting Rebel Assault through its paces was literally all in a day's work. What was unusual was the amount of influence he had over the final game. "It's not necessarily normal for a tester to do the kind of work I did. I kind of took it upon myself to do it, and they were receptive. Vince said, 'Hey, I'm a programmer; you're an avid game player. You know what a difficulty level should be, so here, run with it; I'll help you any way I can.'"

Hardware Hard-Knocks

Chip Hinnenberg, also a key tester on Rebel Assault, concentrated primarily on hardware compatibility issues. "I have an archive of ten CD-ROM drives and a whole sound card library—the whole

Chip Hinnenberg focused primarily on hardware compatibility issues.

SoundBlaster line, Pro Spectrum Audio, all of the popular ones on the market. All of the sound cards need to be tested on every IRQ channel, every DMA channel, and every HEX address, and then you have to make sure everything works with every new version of each sound card's driver software."

Chip says he thoroughly tested about ten different cards, but not all of those were directly supported by Rebel Assault. "We always do SoundBlaster and true SoundBlaster compatibles as well as Roland and General Midi."

Chip's sound card collection, used to test Rebel Assault's compatibility with popular sound cards.

Ditto for CD-ROM drives. Notice the VCR and big-screen TV. The setup lets Chip record scenes and/ or bugs to play later for Vince Lee and the assistant programmers.

Even with all of this hardware testing to conduct, Chip managed to do some playtesting as well. "I was testing lead on Rebel Assault at first, but since I'm the technical specialist, I have to be available for all products. I worked side by side with Brett. We'd go along and converse on every issue." One of Chip's suggestions was implemented in the first chapter, Beggar's Canyon.

"You're going through your first training, and at first it was just left-to-right flying. I hated that, because," Chip says, "there was no sensation of really flying. When you turn left and pull back and bank around a corner, you need to have a sense of feeling that 'tug'." It's effects like this, which Chip calls "crowd pleasers," that keep players interested in the game.

Brett Tosti puts Rebel Assault for the Sega CD through its paces.

Wayne Cline provided additional testing.

Joystick control was one of the elements that Q/A felt needed improvement in the game.

Additional Q/A testing was provided by Dana Fong. Here he tests Rebel Assault for the Macintosh.

Dana also tested Macintosh peripherals for playability and control.

Additional Q/A testers Dana Fong, William Burns, and Dan Connors.

The level Chip is most proud of influencing occurs at the game's climactic ending.

"You're in the trench run. At first, a grid came up and had a target thing that came down, but targeting was too slow and by the time you targeted you were gone." The targeting system Chip says he and Vince devised, after spending several hours working with different colors and grid patterns, is the one that made it into the final game.

Suspension of Disbelief

As a *Star Wars* aficionado, though, Chip does have one small criticism of the game. "If you think about it, some of these things wouldn't work.

A TIE fighter flying in gravity?

Star Wars models from the Lucasfilm archives: an X-wing...

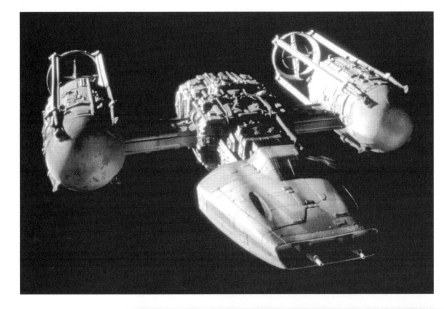

...a Y-wing...

**...and an
Imperial Star
Destroyer.**

A TIE fighter flying in gravity?" he says with a laugh. "Well, a TIE fighter doesn't have wings, only engines on back. When it hit gravity, there wouldn't be anything holding it up, like on the planet where Hack dies. Shuttles, X-wings—they have wings and engines—and the assault gunboats—those actually lift like Harrier jump jets and can take off from anywhere. But TIE fighters flying in gravity...?"

Special Effects

As with those anti-gravity TIEs, every now and then the designers had to bend a few rules, do a few tricks, in order to make something fly. Or crash.

Which is exactly what the art department did at the eleventh hour to create the game's spectacular death scenes, which detonate whenever the player's damage meter peaks. Creating death scenes for each level was no easy feat. Aaron Muszalski says the team managed to get the job done in record time by employing a number of Hollywood-style special effects.

Ron Lussier describes a trick he used: "Rather than create whole new backgrounds and such, the death scenes cannibalize other shots."

Highlighting the scene in which the player's X-wing crashes into an asteroid, Rich Green explains: "I just took an asteroid from an actual playable sequence, then inserted the ship so that it looked like it was getting hit with the asteroid." Sounds simple, but Aaron says there was more to it than just cutting and pasting graphics. "He was using wax pencils to actually mark on his monitor where the asteroid appeared in the frame. Then in 3-D he used those marks to line up where he was trying to make the explosion occur."

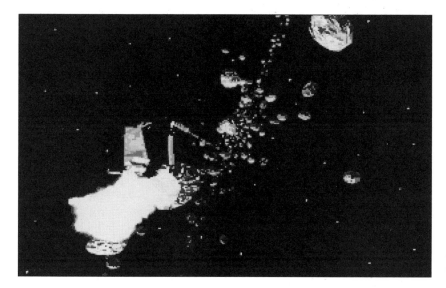

Rebel Assault's "Death Scenes"
were among the last artworks to
be created by the 3-D artists.

The Big Bang

Ron Lussier divulges the technique that is, along with cannibalizing shots, perhaps the game's biggest, yet most subtle, secret: "There's pretty much one explosion in the entire game." By taking the animated explosion and reversing it, flipping it left or right, and resizing it, the artists were able to create several different explosions. At the game's fiery finale, says Ron, "the Death Star has four different elements in that explosion—different sizes, different color palettes—and they go off at different times."

Richard Green used a special
four-layer explosion effect to
blow up the Death Star at the
game's finale.

Thanks to this kind of clever trickery, the artists managed to get the death scenes done in a week-and-a-half. If they hadn't gotten them done so quickly, the game would have shipped without death scenes.

The Player Is Listening

Another team that took advantage of ILM's special effects goodies was the sound and music department, which produced Rebel Assault's spectacular sound effects and musical score.

"We came in unusually late," says Sound Manager Michael Land. "They didn't really use much material generated by us because they licensed the London Symphony score from *Star Wars* and sound effects from Skywalker Sound," the Lucas Digital division that creates sound effects for blockbuster Hollywood films.

Sound Editing and Processing Engineer Clint Bajakian, who did most of Rebel Assault's hands-on sound editing and processing, explains: "This is a real departure, definitely. What we tend to do is meet with project leaders at a game's inception, see what kind of style they want, and then

Sound and music guys, from left to right: Peter McConnell, Clint Bajakian, and Michael Land.

Clint Bajakian created sound effects and music in his studio office.

confer among ourselves. Then one of us can start a piece, get it roughed out, and hand it off to one of the other guys and they'll finish it." Peter McConnell, the third member of the group, also acted as a sound advisor on the project. Because Rebel Assault was to use the film soundtrack, however, Michael says that the trio, coming in toward the end of the project as they did, primarily refined what Vince had figured out on his own.

"It was a combo effort. Vince took it 90 percent of the way. He went through the original CD soundtrack and selected the sections that he liked for each scene. He had a great instinct for how to match the music to the game. We came in near the end, made a few suggestions here and there, then took over the process."

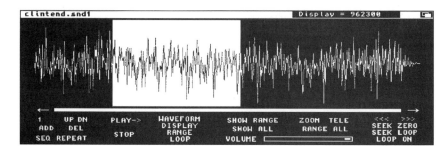

Vince Lee manipulated Rebel Assault's music and sound effects with an Amiga personal computer.

Low-Tech, High-Impact

Clint says Vince's involvement in the process taught the sound team an important lesson.

Vince used a very low-tech process to digitize music from the CD and create the working musical score he gave to the sound team to use as a blueprint. He used a boom box and connected the headphone out line to a simple converter box. "He had no control," says Clint, "over the amount of amplitude on that headphone signal."

Nevertheless, Vince's crude method was not without merit. "Although it sounded overbearing and too powerful, when we were finally charged to produce the music in the 'correct' way—the way you would normally do audio—his music, in an A vs. B comparison, was punchy, present, and visceral, while mine sounded puny, clean, tinny, and trivial. We realized that we had to somehow punch up the signal and achieve distortion on purpose."

Clint says it took him three whole days to achieve the powerful resonance of Vince's sample by adjusting signal volumes to produce greater emphasis in certain parts, less in others.

Using SMUSH, Vince Lee incorporated the sound and music guys' work into the game.

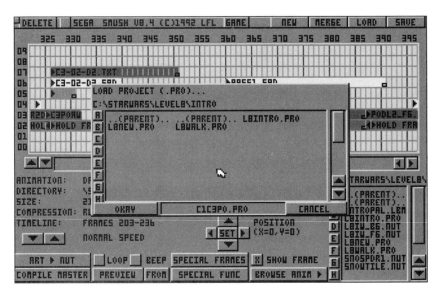

Sound Effects City

Peter extracted the sound effects—from laser blasts to R2-D2's startled scream—from Skywalker Sound's sound effects library, which he calls "a very rare and precious resource." Vince processed the sound effects in SMUSH, which is why, Clint says, "his are very robust, big and rich, and our music is tighter and cleaner and brighter," which he feels is appropriate for the game, considering its emphasis on action. The audio element of SMUSH, like all of its other components, was designed and programmed by Vince. Says Clint, "It's his own creation—a multitrack digital playback system with up to four channels. One is for music, another for voice or radio, and the remaining two for overlapping sound effects. That was really pretty revolutionary in this industry. A lot of games still only have one channel of digital audio, and when a new sound interrupts one that is already playing, it gets cut off, and here Vince comes along and does this four-channel digital system in SMUSH that lets him just drag the elements—both audio and video—around."

John Williams's *Star Wars* soundtrack was used to create all of Rebel Assault's music. Lucas Digital's Skywalker Sound group provided the sound and music department with recorded sound effects taken from the *Star Wars* trilogy of films.

Michael says that Vince's method of handling music and sound effects in Rebel Assault has influenced the way the department will handle those elements in the future. "What it comes down to is that Rebel Assault broke a lot of ground. Pete and I and Justin [Graham], who are responsible for evolving IMUSE [the interactive music system used for the game's graphic adventure titles] have had to readjust our priorities. What we want to do now is digital mixing, which has opened a Pandora's box—streamed digital music, which is not played on synthesizer hardware but rather streamed right off the CD. That's something we've been really seriously trying to pursue. Vince took a very big step. The fallout is that we've all been unambiguously convinced to take the next step. Before Vince did that, we had a lot of debate—it's a pain in the neck—but now we're going to do it as fast as we can, because, boy, it's going to be great!"

Speak Loud and Clear

What the sound team also polished before turning it over to Vince was the game's spoken dialog, which Voice Producer and Director Tamlynn Barra produced by casting and recording professional voice actors.

"I collaborated with Vince first," says Tamlynn, describing the process. "I gave him feedback, like a dialog coach, to make the script more readable

Tamlynn Barra,
Voice Producer and Director

Bill Farmer, who has spoken on behalf of Disney characters Goofy and Pluto...

...and Nick Jameson, who appeared in the film *Robin Hood: Men in Tights*, were two of the actors Tamlynn cast as voice talent for Rebel Assault.

for recording, to make it more natural, tighten it up. The script was done when he froze dialog, then it was ready to go to casting. Next, I auditioned the people. We have a pool of known talent we draw from, but we consider new talent too."

Tamlynn says that 90 percent of the production was done in Los Angeles, in a small studio. "I went down there last September, recorded everything on DAT [Digital Audio Tape], cut it out, and edited it, did the processing on it, and gave it to the sound and music department, which gave it to Vince, who hacked it all into the game. The engine for Rebel Assault had to do lip synching manually, so he tried to tweak it as closely as he could."

Clint Bajakian says that when he received the 16-bit recordings from Tamlynn, he broke them down and equalized them to make them sound as clean as possible. For the "radio chatter," portions, he did a few tricks to add a stronger sense of realism. "The way to achieve that radio chatter effect is by narrowing the bandwidth in the middle to high end, which gives it a staticky kind of trebly walkie-talkie sound, like the telephone."

Market Measures

Speaking of the telephone, Marketing Director Mary Bihr and Public Relations Manager Sue Seserman were, among other things, busy getting out the word that Rebel Assault was on its way to market and were finalizing the product's package design. Much of the package design was determined by the game's position in the company's existing product line. Mary explains: "The press started picking up on rumors that there was this CD-ROM product based on *Star Wars*, and the speculation was that it would be the CD version of X-Wing," the company's best-selling disk-based space combat simulator. "We thought, 'Oh my gosh, we have to make sure the perception is really, really clear.' So Vince and I locked ourselves in a room and threw a bunch of names on a whiteboard that were not vehicle names, because our space sim games were all named after vehicles, and our cartridge games were named after the movies.

"We had three other properties in stores—for the SNES there was Super Empire Strikes Back and Star Wars, and for PC's the whole X-Wing series. Then there was this crazy product called Rebel Assault, our first CD-ROM product." Differentiating the products was a challenge. "The strategy was clear for flight sims—photo realistic segments from the game on the package, in contrast to the cartridge-based games, which are character-based, side-scrolling games. We differentiated those from X-Wing

Mary Bihr, LucasArts Director of Marketing, and Sue Seserman, Public Relations Manager

PART THREE   THE CRUNCH

by showing a montage, harking back to the movie poster, depicting major areas of action in the game and major characters—Luke, Han, Chewie, Leia." With those angles already taken, Mary says, they had to do something totally new for Rebel Assault. "It called for brighter colors than our other games, a brighter logo, and something that would appeal across platforms. There was a lot of argument even after the boxes were printed. Some people said it looked too 'action-arcade,' too 'kid-like,' and my argument was it was an action-arcade game, and it had to work in both markets, PC CD-ROM and Sega CD, so you pick the best for both and

Rebel Assault is shown here beside additional LucasArts *Star Wars* games: X-Wing for PC computers and Super Empire Strikes Back for Super Nintendo.

The Rebel Assault original illustration used for the product's packaging.

73

Lisa Star, International Administrator, coordinated Rebel Assault's foreign releases, including...

...the German package...

...and the Chinese package.

try to set design parameters around that. Up until the last minute, we were wondering if we had made the right choice with the Superman colors—red and blue and yellow—but it all worked out in the end."

Sue says that getting out the message that Rebel Assault was the company's first game designed exclusively for CD-ROM was one of her biggest concerns. "It was a big selling point and one that helped to differentiate it from other games out there, particularly X-Wing. That was something we were able to accomplish largely through PR because we could literally spell it out in a press release. Vince explained the technology to me, and he worked closely with me to put the press release together using technical and story highlights."

**Public Relations Associate
Camela Boswell and
Sue Seserman at work.**

The Final Stretch

With so many people and departments involved in the project—from Q/A to sound and music to voice recording to marketing and public relations—Vince was being pulled in many directions as the ship date drew nearer. Having dedicated two years of his life to the project, often working nights and weekends, he was starting to burn out.

**Vince Lee, plugging along:
"The last two months of the
project were intense."**

"The last three months of the project were very post-production intense," Vince says. "That's when lots of art and voices and recordings started coming in. The last two months were completely haywire. At the very end of the game, we were doing post-production, and we didn't get the final art until a month before that. We did all the post-production on the last few levels in a month and a half."

The Calvary

To allow Vince to focus on getting the game finished rather than dealing with a multitude of administrative details, Steve Dauterman brought in Casey Donahue Ackley as associate producer of the product.

"Steve asked me to come in to Rebel Assault and try to rally everyone together and manage the crisis. Vince had many responsibilities— programming, designing, and project-leading. He just didn't have time to keep checking on the art department or deal with marketing." It was Casey's job to see to it that everything went smoothly during the final high-tension push to complete the project. "My duties were managing— making sure the art guys knew what Vince wanted, making sure Vince knew what the art guys wanted. I had to take the art list and rearrange it, prioritize it, check with Vince every few hours and re-prioritize shots.

Associate Producer Casey Donahue Ackley and her Rebel Assault production binder.

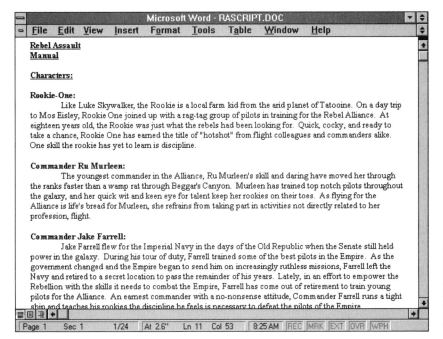

In her role as overseer of Rebel Assault's final production phase, Casey wrote the Rebel Assault manual (shown here in its original text format) with Vince's assistance.

It was a grueling job to get it out by November first. Vince worked something like 20-hour days. I don't know if he slept. His heart and soul and blood were in that game, and the artists and testers all put in really long hours too."

In addition, Casey wrote the Rebel Assault manual with Vince's help. "I'd write something and take it to Vince and he'd change things." She also put together the reference card, which reflected last minute changes in the game that were not included in the manual.

Toward the end of the project, when tensions were at their highest and patience at its lowest, the Rebel Assault team began to be rejuvenated by the advance good will the product was garnering. At the Summer '93 CES, where the game was announced, members of the press were, according to Sue Seserman, "bowled over by the realism of the 3-D graphics, the full-screen video, the digital soundtrack with John Williams's score, the speech, and so forth. A lot of these things either hadn't been done before or had been integrated crudely in the past."

At the same time, a demo is just that, a demonstration of a product—not the real thing. Was anyone worried? "Nobody thought it was going to be horrible or an embarrassment to the company," says Steve Dauterman, "but how do you top a product like X-Wing, which everyone was saying was the top of the heap?" If the response Casey received when she showed the product to an unsuspecting audience just before it shipped was any indication, topping the top of the heap was just around the corner.

Seeing Is Believing

"I was asked to bring Rebel Assault to the Mill Valley Film Festival. I'd never done a public demo before, and I was really bad at demonstrating Rebel Assault because I hadn't had a lot of time to play the game. I was one of the last presenters in a series of six, and it was a huge audience of all kinds of multimedia and film people. The other products shown ranged from artsy titles that were slow and beautiful to sports games and an 'out-there' underwater exploration." Then it was Casey's turn at the podium. "I started with the title *Star Wars* screen and blasted the theme song, and the whole audience started laughing because they had heard something familiar! They were cheering as I was trying to maneuver through the canyon and got excited when I made it to the stormtrooper level. We'd been looking at all these gorgeous programs and experiments, and here

Casey is also Associate Producer for the FM Towns, Macintosh, and Sega CD version (shown here) of Rebel Assault.

was a shoot-'em-up game that didn't belong at the conference at all. The crowd went wild. The guy after me, the last presenter, said, 'Now I know why I'm going to buy a CD-ROM player,' and he tried to buy the beta CD-ROM of Rebel Assault I was playing."

Destiny Awaits

Vince Lee tells his own pre-ship-date story, this one a little more intimate: "Halfway through the development process, I brought in a friend of mine who was not into computer games. I had all the place-holder art in there, and she looked at it and told me later that she was not impressed. It wasn't until a month before release that I showed it to her again. She said, 'Oh wow!'"

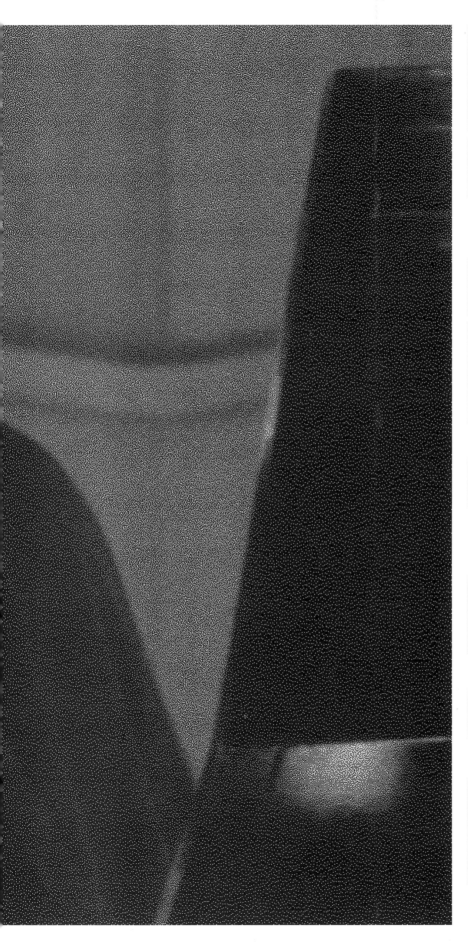

EPILOGUE

Rebel Invasion

"OH WOW!" INDEED. Rebel Assault hit store shelves in mid-November. It was an overnight success—a colossal OH WOW!, you might say. It is the best-selling CD-ROM game in history; at last count, the company had shipped more than 600,000 copies of the game, and demand hasn't cooled one bit. And that's not counting the Macintosh and Sega CD versions.

End of story, right?

Not quite. Amanda Haverlock, LucasArts's genial receptionist, explains: "November hit, Rebel Assault came out, then 'BOOM,' my job changed—from piddling around trying to find something to do to constantly being on the phone. The tech support lines were swamped, jam-packed, and people couldn't get through on those lines, so they got me. My phone would ring constantly all day long—mostly calls for help or to order the game."

"Mrs. Doubtfire, Calling"

One call took her completely by surprise. "Robin Williams called once, and I got to talk to him. I didn't recognize his voice at first; I thought it was a friend of mine. He was calling about Rebel Assault. He said he and his son were playing, and he wanted to talk to Vince for some hints. I told him how much I loved *Mrs. Doubtfire*. He was really flattered!"

Amanda Haverlock, LucasArts receptionist.

Trouble in Paradise

What wasn't flattering for the company was that it was totally unprepared for Rebel Assault's phenomenal success and the demand it placed on the Product Support Department, which, at the time, consisted of only four people.

Mara Kaehn, Product Support Manager, describes what went down. "After it shipped, our calls were moderate to heavy. We were here during Thanksgiving weekend, and they were pretty heavy then," because, Mara explains, young players were home from school for the Thanksgiving holiday. Ditto for Christmas, which is when things really heated up. "It started a week before Christmas. Then the day after Christmas, it was incredible. We were getting so many calls and faxes we were running out of fax paper every half hour—that's two hundred sheets. We had so many faxes lined up we had to have temps come in to separate them and reply, 'Don't send us another fax—we'll get back to you.' People in the group were hiding under their desks. They were so stressed out, always looking run down—it was awful."

Some callers were complaining that the game was crashing on their systems. LucasArts traced the problem to a third-party system software

Mara Kaehn,
Product Support Manager.

component the game uses to manage the computer's extended memory, enabling it to exceed DOS's usual 640K conventional memory limit. Responding quickly, the company created and started sending out a "patch disk," which rectified the crashing problem. The patch was also posted on CompuServe, America Online, Genie, and LucasArts's own Bulletin Board System (BBS), so customers who owned modems could download it and use it at once, rather than wait for the patch disk to arrive by mail.

Techie Turn-Off

By and large, however, most of the calls the Product Support staff received (and still receive) had to do with setting up users' config.sys and autoexec.bat files. The instructions included with the game explain how to create a boot disk that allows the computer to boot without using the hard disk when Rebel Assault is played. But, as the Product Support staff will tell you, many users are unfamiliar with system configuration issues such as these, so they call the company to be walked through the boot disk creation process one step at a time. And call they did.

Mara says that many users reported that they were so excited by Rebel Assault that not only was it the first game they ever purchased but it also

Jason Deadrich, Lead Technical Coordinator.

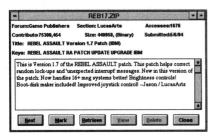

The Product Support Department posted software patches to fix glitches in the game on CompuServe (shown here), America Online, Genie, and LucasArts's own bulletin board system.

prompted them to purchase their first CD-ROM drive. Which explains why users—a great many of whom typically run pre-loaded Windows applications only—are afraid of going under the hood and messing with cryptic DOS configuration files.

Giving Users the Boot

What did LucasArts do to solve the problem? "One day," Mara says, "I talked to one of the development guys. I said, 'We really needed to include a boot disk maker with Rebel Assault.'" A boot disk maker is a program that automatically formats a blank disk for the user and creates the necessary autoexec.bat and config.sys files onto it so the player can then used it to boot his or her system and play the game. Mara submitted a "sensitivity report," which detailed how much money she thought the company was losing, based on the number of frustrated users she estimated were returning the game to stores because they couldn't get it to run on their computers. A boot disk maker, she concluded, would go a long way toward solving the problem.

The boot disk maker is now included with the latest version of Rebel Assault and in the latest patch, which is available on America Online, CompuServe, Delphi, and LucasArts's own BBS.

```
                  LucasArts Entertainment Co.
                   Game Boot Disk Utility v1.07
               Copyright (c)1994, LucasArts Entertainment Co.

This program creates a floppy disk that you can use to boot your
computer. This "boot disk" should enable you to run some of our
games more efficiently and effectively.

This program will:
1st : Read the AUTOEXEC.BAT and CONFIG.SYS files that are currently
on your computer.

2nd : Format a system disk on drive A.

3rd : It will copy certain lines in your current AUTOEXEC.BAT and
CONFIG.SYS files to new AUTOEXEC.BAT and CONFIG.SYS files. These new
files will be placed on your new "boot disk".


Do you want to make a boot disk (Y/N)?
```

Responding to an overwhelming number of calls regarding autoexec.bat and config.sys file conflicts, Product Support spearheaded the creation of a "boot disk maker," which automatically creates a boot disk for players' computers.

Bigger, Better Support

The product has changed since it began shipping and so has the entire Product Support staff—due largely to Rebel Assault's popularity and the demand it has placed on the staff. Mara explains: "We have 16 people now and a new phone system," which can direct callers to certain topics and queue overflow calls on hold. They have also added "an expert help system on our computers that lets us log a call, time it, figure out what the

Product Support's digs before Rebel Assault...

...and after the product shipped. The group has grown from four people to sixteen.

problem is, get data back, and solve problems." To accommodate its increased size, the staff has moved into a new building across the street from LucasArts headquarters, and each Product Support specialist now has his or her own PC, which replaces the former paper-based "solutions" binders they used to use to help callers solve problems. The group has also taken delivery of several Macintosh computers to help them answer questions they receive on that version of Rebel Assault. Another thing that has changed is that the Product Support group is now involved in product development during the Q/A process. "Now there's a little check-off box in testing," Mara says, "which looks at the product from the customer's point of view, for things they think we'll get calls on, like

LucasArts titles and hint books close at hand to the Product Support staff.

The Product Support cork board bears the latest news and info on games, the business, and staying healthy in the age of computers.

LucasArts hint line experts
Tabitha Tosti...

...and Kim
Gresko.

something that's confusing. They'll mark that, and I get that information from Mark [Cartwright] and create a list of product support concerns." With that information, the development staff may make changes in the product so that it works differently or is easier to install.

With future games, the company intends to include a new and improved configuration utility that makes it easier for users to set up their systems. The first game to include the utility is TIE Fighter, which features an "express" setup option that automatically detects what kind of hardware—processor, sound board, memory, video, etc.—the user has and then configures the game for correct and optimal playability.

Who's Playing?

In addition to the valuable product support lessons the company has learned, Rebel Assault has provided LucasArts's Product Marketing Manager, Barbara Gleason, with a revealing portrait of the customers who are buying and playing the game. Having received the results of a customer satisfaction survey she recently conducted, Barbara says some of the findings are quite surprising.

"Based on registration cards, an outside firm calls customers and asks them questions about Rebel Assault, CD-ROM entertainment, preferences, and so on. We found out a lot of interesting things."

Barbara Gleason, LucasArts Product Marketing Manager, conducted a recent study to analyze Rebel Assault's success.

Boys Will Be Boys

At the top of the list, she learned that "players are overwhelmingly (99 percent) male, which is the highest I've ever seen for any of our games." As for player age, "Rebel Assault has universal appeal among ages. One-third are under 20, one-third are between 20 and 35, and one third are over 36 years old." She says that the company positioned the game as family entertainment, and it turned out to be exactly that. "Sixty percent of all Rebel households have more than one player. It seems that most— 70 percent—are heavy users of floppy-based PC games. The remaining 20 to 30 percent were probably new PC owners and light gamers—the ones who were calling Product Support for help."

As for players' reaction to the company's first game designed exclusively for CD-ROM, players said that they "loved CD-ROM games and plan on purchasing quite a few."

Favorites and Not-So Favorites

Questions about the Rebel Assault's features yielded equally surprising results. From a list of points, players rated features from most important to least important. At the top of the list were 3-D graphics. Sound and music came in second place, and full-screen video took third. As for how Rebel Assault ranked against other popular CD-ROMs selling at the time of the survey, 93 percent rated Rebel Assault as their favorite.

"Players are overwhelmingly male: 99 percent."

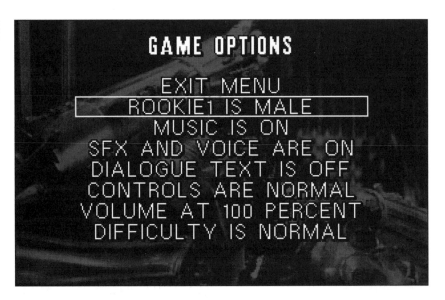

Rebel Assault—Part Deux?

With results like those, can Rebel Assault—The Sequel be far off? LucasArts isn't saying.

Meanwhile, Vince Lee seems awfully busy, and some very *Star Wars*-like sounds—sounds that assuredly are not those we listened to in the original Rebel Assault—are emanating from his office.

Hey, Vince, where are you going with that joystick in your hand?

To be continued…

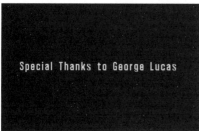

George Lucas, to whom the Rebel Assault team gave a special thanks in the game's credits…

…sent the team this congratulatory letter after the game shipped.

Credits

Special Thanks to George Lucas

Based on *Star Wars* by George Lucas

DESIGNER, PROGRAMMER, PROJECT LEADER

Vince Lee

LEAD 3D ARTIST-ANIMATOR

Ron Lussier

VOICE PRODUCER AND DIRECTOR

Tamlynn Barra

ASSOCIATE GAME PRODUCER

Casey Donahue Ackley

3D ARTIST–ANIMATORS

David Vallone

Richard Green

ADDITIONAL 3-D ART BY

Ralph Gerth

Dan Colon Jr.

Steven Sherer

3-D MODELERS

Martin Cameron

Jon Bell

ARTIST–ANIMATORS

Leonard Robel

Bill Tiller

ADDITIONAL ART

Larry Ahern

Jon Knoles

John Knoll

LEAD ART TECHNICIAN

Aaron Muszalski

ART TECHNICIANS

Chris Ross

Leyton Chew

Gwen Musengwa

QUALITY ASSURANCE SUPERVISOR

Mark Cartwright

QUALITY ASSURANCE AND COMPATIBILITY TESTING

Chip Hinnenberg

Brett Tosti

Dana Fong

ADDITIONAL TESTING

Matthew Forbush

William Burns

Chris Purvis

MACINTOSH PROGRAMMER

Eric Johnson

FM TOWNS PROGRAMMER

Paul LeFerve

PROGRAMMING ASSISTANCE

Justin Graham

Toshi Morita

Mark Haigh-Hutchinson

Edward Kilham

Aric Wilmunder

Gary Brubaker

SOUND EDITING AND PROCESSING

Clint Bajakian

SOUND ADVICE

Michael Z. Land

Peter McConnell

ART DEPARTMENT DIRECTOR

Collette Michaud

PUBLIC RELATIONS MANAGER

Sue Seserman

DISTRIBUTION MANAGER

Meredith Cahill

PRODUCT SUPPORT SUPERVISOR

Mara Kaehn

INTERNATIONAL COORDINATOR

Lisa Star

DIRECTOR OF MARKETING

Mary Bihr

DIRECTOR OF PRODUCTION

Steve Dauterman

DIRECTOR OF BUSINESS OPERATIONS

Jack Sorensen

VOICE TALENT

Nick Jameson

Bill Farmer

Denny Delk

Tony Pope

and

Ru Murleen as herself

SPECIAL THANKS TO

Collette Michaud	Peter Chan
Tamlynn Barra	Mike Levine
Steve Purcell	Jack Sorensen
Justin Graham	Jon Levinson
Hal Barwood	Mary Fitzgerald
Wayne Cline	Jonathan Ackley
Jon Knoles	Casey Donahue Ackley

Original *Star Wars* Soundtrack Music

Performed by the London Symphony Orchestra

Composed and Conducted by John Williams

(P) © 1977 Lucasfilm Ltd.

Used Under Authorization. All Rights Reserved.

Index

F

Farmer, Bill, 71

Film soundtrack, 66–67

FM Towns version, 52

Fong, Dana, 61

Full-screen video, 90

G

Game engine, 7

Game play, 53

   challenge of, 56

   development of, 57–58

   testing for, 55–56

General Midi, 59

Genie, patch disk on, 84

German packaging, 74

Gerth, Ralph, 54

GIF2DXF, 27–28

Gleason, Barbara, 89

Graham, Justin, 52, 70

Graphics. *See* 3-D graphics

Green, Richard, 31, 32

   on compression issue, 43

   cut scenes, 37

   explosion effect, 65

Gresko, Kim, 88

H

Hack, Lt. Turland, 40, 63

Haigh-Hutchinson, Mark, 53

Hard game play, 57–58

Hardware compatibility, 58–60

Harris, Rookie Thurlow, 41

Haverlock, Amanda, 82

Help system, 86–87

HEX addresses, 59

Hinnenberg, Chip, 58–63

Hoth orbit of Imperial Star Destroyer, 34

I

Imperial Star Destroyers, 23, 26, 63

   dogfight sequence, 30

   Hoth orbit of, 34

   TIE fighters relative to, 45

Imperial Walkers, 24, 25

   Luke Skywalker perspective of, 26

IMUSE, 70

Indiana Jones and the Fate of Atlantis, 3

Industrial Light and Magic (ILM), 13

International marketing, 74

Interpolation, 31

IRQ channels, 59

Secrets of the Games

NOW AVAILABLE FROM PRIMA

Computer Game Books

SimEarth: The Official Strategy Guide	$19.95
Harpoon Battlebook: The Official Strategy Guide	$19.95
The Official Lucasfilm Games Air Combat Strategies Book	$19.95
Sid Meier's Civilization, or Rome on 640K a Day	$19.95
Wing Commander I and II: The Ultimate Strategy Guide	$19.95
Chuck Yeager's Air Combat Handbook	$19.95
Ultima: The Avatar Adventures	$19.95
A-Train: The Official Strategy Guide	$19.95
PowerMonger: The Official Strategy Guide	$19.95
Global Conquest: The Official Strategy Guide (with disk)	$24.95
Gunship 2000: The Official Strategy Guide	$19.95
Dynamix Great War Planes: The Ultimate Strategy Guide	$19.95
SimLife: The Official Strategy Guide	$19.95
Populous: The Official Strategy Guide	$19.95
Stunt Island: The Official Strategy Guide	$19.95
Ultima VII and Underworld: More Avatar Adventures	$19.95
X-Wing: The Official Strategy Guide	$19.95
Prince of Persia: The Official Strategy Guide	$19.95
Empire Deluxe: The Official Strategy Guide	$19.95
F-15 Strike Eagle III: The Official Strategy Guide (with disk)	$24.95
Lemmings: The Official Companion (with disk)	$24.95
Secret of Mana Official Game Secrets	$14.95
The 7th Guest: The Official Strategy Guide	$19.95
Myst: The Official Strategy Guide	$19.95
Return to Zork Adventurer's Guide	$14.95
Microsoft Flight Simulator: The Official Strategy Guide	$19.95
Strike Commander: The Official Strategy Guide and Flight School	$19.95
Might and Magic Compendium: The Authorized Strategy Guide for Games I, II, III, and IV	$19.95
SimFarm Almanac: The Official Guide to SimFarm	$19.95
Computer Adventure Games Secrets	$19.95
Quest for Glory: The Authorized Strategy Guide	$19.95
Falcon 3: The Official Combat Strategy Book, revised ed.	$19.95
SimCity 2000: Power, Politics, and Planning	$19.95
SSN-21 Seawolf: The Official Strategy Guide	$19.95
Master of Orion: The Official Strategy Guide	$19.95
Outpost: The Official Strategy Guide	$19.95
Betrayal at Krondor: The Official Strategy Guide	$19.95
Alone in the Dark: The Official Strategy Guide	$19.95
Dracula Unleashed: The Official Strategy Guide & Novel	$19.95
CD-ROM Games Secrets, Volume 1	$19.95
Sherlock Holmes, Consulting Detective: The Unauthorized Strategy Guide	$19.95
Pagan: Ultima VIII—The Ultimate Strategy Guide	$19.95
Rebel Assault: The Official Insider's Guide	$19.95

Video Game Books

Nintendo Games Secrets, Volumes 1, 2, 3, and 4	$12.95	each
Nintendo Game Boy Secrets, Volumes 1 and 2	$12.95	each
TurboGrafx-16 and TurboExpress Secrets, Volumes 1 and 2	$11.95	each
GamePro Presents: Nintendo Games Secrets Greatest Tips	$11.95	
GamePro Presents: Sega Genesis Games Secrets Greatest Tips	$11.95	
Super Mario World Game Secrets	$12.95	
The Legend of Zelda: A Link to the Past—Game Secrets	$12.95	
Sega Genesis Secrets, Volumes 1, 2, 3, and 4	$12.95	each
Sega Genesis and Sega CD Secrets, Volume 5	$12.95	
Super Star Wars: The Official Strategy Guide	$12.95	
Official Sega Genesis Power Tips Book, 2nd Edition (in full color!)	$14.95	
GamePro Presents: Super NES Games Secrets Greatest Tips, Second Edition	$12.95	
Super NES Games Secrets, Volumes 1, 2, 3, and 4	$12.95	each
Super Empire Strikes Back Official Game Secrets	$12.95	
Super NES Games Unauthorized Power Tips Book	$14.95	
Battletoads: The Official Battlebook	$12.95	
Parent's Guide to Video Games	$12.95	
Sega Genesis Games Secrets Greatest Tips, Second Edition	$12.95	
Sega Genesis Games Secrets Greatest Tips, Second Edition	$12.95	
Sega Mega Drive Games Secrets Greatest Tips, Second Edition	$12.95	
Sega Genesis Games Secrets, Volume 6	$12.95	
Sega CD Official Game Secrets	$12.95	
Eternal Champions Power Tips Book	$9.95	

To Order Books

Please send me the following items:

Quantity #	Title	Unit Price	Total
_____	_____	$ _____	$ _____
_____	_____	$ _____	$ _____
_____	_____	$ _____	$ _____
_____	_____	$ _____	$ _____
_____	_____	$ _____	$ _____
_____	_____	$ _____	$ _____

Subtotal $ _____

7.25% Sales Tax (California only) $ _____

Shipping and Handling* $ _____

Total Order $ _____

*$4.00 shipping and handling charge for the first book and $0.50 for each additional book.

BY TELEPHONE: With Visa or MC, call (916) 632-4400 Mon.–Fri., 9–4 PST.
BY MAIL: Just fill out the information below and send with your remittance to:

Prima Publishing
P.O. Box 1260BK
Rocklin, CA 95677

Satisfaction unconditionally guaranteed

My name is _____

I live at _____

City _____ State _____ Zip _____

MC/Visa # _____ Exp. _____

Signature _____